HOW TO BEAT THE MARKET WITH HIGH-PERFORMANCE GENERIC STOCKS*

*YOUR BROKER WON'T TELL YOU ABOUT

HOW TO BEAT THE MARKET WITH HIGH-PERFORMANCE GENERIC STOCKS*

*YOUR BROKER WON'T TELL YOU ABOUT

Avner Arbel, M.B.A., Ph.D.
Professor of Finance Cornell University

William Morrow and Company, Inc. New York

To my family
whose prominent desire
for brand-name products
made the Generic Stock Investment Strategy
NECESSARY

Library of Congress Cataloging in Publication Data

Arbel, Avner, 1935–
  How to beat the market with high-performance
generic stocks*   *your broker won't tell you about

  Includes index.
  1. Speculation. 2. Investments. I. Title.
HG6036.A73 1985   332.63'22   85-2886
ISBN 0-688-04371-2

Printed in the United States of America

2 3 4 5 6 7 8 9 10

BOOK DESIGN BY PATTY LOWY

Acknowledgments

The research on the Neglected Firm Effect that led to this book was started in 1977 at the School of Management, State University of New York at Binghamton and continued later at Cornell University. Dozens of people have been involved; colleagues, research assistants, computer programmers, Ph.D. candidates, and many students. I truly thank them all. Together we coped with huge data bases and had our share of "Bang Bang Solutions" and good days.

One person, more than anybody else, deserves thanks for everything that brought this book to existence: Dr. Paul J. Strebel, previously at SUNY Binghamton and now at I.M.E.D.E.Management Development Institute, Lausanne, Switzerland. I worked with Paul on the Neglected Firm Effect project from its inception. Together we came up with the initial ideas and for years struggled to test and refine them.

Paul, a brilliant thinker and a true intellectual, inspired my thinking throughout. But he did more than that. He is the most positive, open-minded, and constructive skeptic that one can ask for; the kind needed for any research. His smart response to the continuing flow of new ideas helped keep things under control. He always forced us to sharpen our arguments, and to test and retest. One cannot find a better research partner to work with. Thanks, Paul.

Special thanks are also due to Irene Reiss, now with B.E.A. Associates, and Dr. Steve Carvell. Their excellent research projects contributed a lot.

Cindy Kester successfully translated our ideas into computer programs and produced mountains of Zebra computer printouts. Her careful and innovative approach to programming makes her not only an excellent programmer but also a capable experiment designer. We were lucky to have Cindy on our team for so long.

I also want to express my thanks to Institutional Brokers Estimate System (I.B.E.S.) and Zack's Investment Research for giving us access to their large computerized data bases.

Dr. Charles Bishoff helped us throughout with econometric and statistical advice, and his careful critique on an early draft of the book helped to strengthen several weak areas.

Thanks are also due to the editor of the *Financial Analysts Journal,* Dr. Charles D'Ambrosio; the editor of the *Financial Review,* Dr. James Boness; and the editor of the *Journal of Portfolio Management,* Dr. Peter L. Berenstien, as well as the anonymous referees for their valuable suggestions and comments.

I also want to acknowledge helpful comments from my colleagues at Cornell: Professors Toby Berger, Leo Renaghan, Bill Kaven, and Francine Herman, and Dean Jack Clark of the Cornell School of Hotel Administration for continuous support.

I owe a special thanks to Deborah Knight, who checked early drafts and repeatedly called my attention to grammatical and structural problems. Her sharp editorial work made this book more readable.

I have been lucky to have Donna Vose as my secretary. She not only carefully typed countless drafts but was concerned with the content and helped with comments that improved the presentation. She never lost control, even at the unavoidable moments of crisis. I am still waiting for her to miss a deadline.

How can one thank a process? Of special importance were the hundreds of nameless students who were critical for developing and testing my ideas with their flood of thoughtful questions, brilliant "thoughts," and endless discussions in and out of the classrooms.

Last but not least, a thank-you goes to Douglas Stumpf, my editor at William Morrow. He believed in the project right from the beginning and gave me excellent critical advice that required a lot of work but improved the presentation considerably.

Since none of the listed above will get any share of the royalties from this book, it is only fair to conclude with the customary statement that responsibility for all remaining errors are mine alone.

Furthermore, since I don't expect any reader to share with me the fruits of the successful implementation of the ideas presented in this book, I also don't expect any complaints should you fail. As the saying goes: It's only in the dictionary that success comes before work. As you will see soon, this is true also for the Generic Stock Investment Strategy. You will have to do your share. I honestly wish you good luck. The reward can be substantial.

Author's Note

In my office at Cornell University there is a poster that I got from some finance book salesman saying: NOBODY CLAIMS THAT FINANCE IS EASY. I hung it there to impress my students and especially my good friends, professors in other fields, who might actually believe it. Actually, the poster is wrong. I truly believe that even finance can be made easy and even fun to explore. This book is a modest attempt in this direction.

I want to apologize to my academic colleagues for using nonacademic jargon and for popularization of some of the concepts. That was all done for the sake of practicality and in order to minimize the sleep-inducing qual ity of technical discussions.

—DR. AVNER ARBEL
Cornell University
Ithaca, N.Y.

Contents

What Is This Book All About?

This book is about how to benefit from an astonishing stock market phenomenon that puzzles academics and practitioners alike: the Neglected Firm Effect.

This recently discovered anomaly refers to the superior performance of neglected stocks that for many years have consistently earned abnormally high returns for investors even after adjusting for the usual measures of risk. Among the puzzling elements of this phenomenon is, not only the magnitude of the returns and the striking implication that it is possible to "beat the market," but, mainly, its persistence over many years, with almost no interruption. Which immediately raises the question: How can this be?

Wall Street is full of orphans. By orphans I mean wallflowers, sleeping beauties, or, as we'll call them, *neglected stocks*. While some of them will stay neglected ever after, others will be adopted and gradually start to follow the popularity flow. They will stop being neglected, and in the process will requite their adopters with a sweet reward. As we shall see, there are good theoretical reasons and hard empirical evidence to suggest that this is the case not only for a few individual neglected stocks but also for the group as a whole.

But what about the perpetual sleepers—stocks that are neglected permanently for good reasons? Surprising as it might sound, evidence shows that a diversified portfolio of neglected stocks selected at random—that is, without even screening them to eliminate the potential losers—outperformed the market as a whole, and significantly so. In fact, neglected stocks *as a group*, including both the gems and the junk, the later-to-bediscovereds and the permanent sleepers, performed extremely well. This astonishing phenomenon is called the Neglected Firm Effect.

What are the practical implications of this effect? If the past can be used as an indication of the future, the message for investors is clear: Invest in neglected stocks.

But this is not the end of the story. It will be shown that when simple screening techniques are used, the Neglected Firm Effect can be made to work even better, even beyond the above-average performance of the neglected group as a whole, resulting in still better performance (higher return, lower risk) for the selected (screened) group of neglected stocks.

At this point, no doubt, many questions are popping into your mind:

—How do you define "neglect"?

—How can one *practically* identify neglected stocks?

—Once identified, what is the most effective investment strategy for benefiting from the Neglected Firm Effect?

—What about risk? Aren't the neglected stocks also more risky?

—Will the outstanding performance persist over time? If everybody knows about the Neglected Firm Effect, won't it disappear once followed? (Maybe this book should be kept secret.)

—Do we have to accept the widely unacceptable notion that the market is inefficient?

—What's so special about being neglected?

—Isn't the Neglected Firm Effect just a redundant reflection of the Small Firm Effect?

—The whole thing sounds like a free lunch—getting something for nothing—which makes no sense.

And the unavoidable question:

—Assuming that the neglected firm investment approach does indeed work, should it be adopted by all investors or perhaps just some? And if so, by whom?

These questions represent well-deserved skepticism. While not easy to answer, they are important and must be dealt with. Without satisfactory answers to these questions, any investment strategy based upon the Neglected Firm Effect will have the value of a solar flashlight. A nice idea—new, interesting, somewhat sophisticated, but useless.

In this book, we will try to answer these questions.

The book is divided into three parts.

The first part is devoted to a presentation of the phenomenon itself: the Neglected Firm Effect as observed in the market, its magnitude and its characteristics. The idea of generic stocks will be presented and explained. We shall start with the what-is-it and does-it-work questions. Results of five years of rigorous academic research will be discussed.* This first part is designed to lay the groundwork. You have to know what we are talking about and have a feel for the magnitude of the neglected firm phenomenon and its characteristics before we proceed with more specific investment techniques.

The second part covers pragmatic application for investors of the concepts of neglected and generic stocks. It deals with the how-to-do-it question: in simple terms,

---

*Most of this research was done together with Professor Paul J. Strebel of the School of Management, State University of New York at Binghamton, with the help of dozens of graduate students and Ph.D. candidates. The research was later continued at Cornell University, and is indebted to I.B.E.S (Institutional Brokers Estimate System) and Zacks Investment Research for supplying the invaluable, huge computerized data bases.

how to make money using this phenomenon. In a step-by-step approach, we shall present, explain, and demonstrate the Generic Stock Investment Strategy. The implications for private investors, small institutional investors, and large financial institutions will be examined. The generic trap and how to avoid it will be discussed, as will the limitations of the generic approach. And most important, we shall see who should and who shouldn't use this approach. (In fact, one objective of this book is to help you to decide whether the whole approach of going generic is for you.)

Finally, in the last part of the book, which some of the most pragmatic readers may choose to skip, the whys will be discussed. That is, the reasons for the Neglected Firm Effect and how it works. How is it related to other market anomalies that are so hard to explain, such as the Small Firm Effect, the January Effect, and the Low P/E Anomaly? And can it help to untangle them? We shall try to understand if, and how, the Neglected Firm Effect can survive over time. We shall discuss market efficiency, investors' rationality, the role of financial institutions in creating the Neglected Firm Effect. We shall cover concepts like information deficiency, the role of consensus in generating the generic premium, greed and fear, popularity flows and their rewards, and many other related topics. In this last part, we shall wander close to the frontier of the market knowledge, asking tough questions and enjoying the challenge of coping with chilling skepticism.

But we shouldn't put the cart before the horse. Let's start now with a guided tour of a gray, disorganized but fascinating segment of the market: the fuzzy territory of neglected stocks. The discussion will be frequently interrupted with doses of "Food for Thought," which may induce you to look at the material in a deeper way or from a different angle.

PART I
THE GENERIC STOCK INVESTMENT STRATEGY: WHAT IS IT AND DOES IT REALLY WORK?

What Are Neglected Stocks?

Before we present the evidence about the outstanding performance of neglected stocks and examine its practical implications for improving investment performance, we first have to describe what we mean by neglect. So, let's get some definitions over with. You probably also wonder what generic stocks are. With this concept, however, you will have to be a bit more patient. There is more to it than meets the eye.

Neglect is a concept that relates to information available about a stock. Ideally, the degree of neglect should be measured by (a) the quantity, (b) the quality, and (c) the convenience and rapidity of obtaining information about the stock in question at a certain time. Thus, conceptually, we can define a neglected stock as one for which not much information is currently available, and for which the little information that is available is of low quality and difficult and time-consuming to get. In reality, however, there is no single measure that explicitly quantifies and ranks neglect as I have just conceptually defined it. Therefore, we have to identify neglected stocks through indirect means.

There are several such indicators, but two are the best, in the sense that they are both capable of effectively identifiying neglected stocks and consequently capturing the Neglected Firm Effect. At the same time, they are practical and easy to use. They also happen to make theoretical sense—a quality not always found for market-related practical measures. The two can be used separately or together as a double check.

The first indicator for neglect is tied to the relative attention that the stock gets. The other measures *actual* investors' behavior. Luckily, but not surprisingly, there is a broad overlap between these two.

According to the first indicator, a stock is neglected if it is not widely and continually followed by security analysts. In our research, which was mostly done with Professor Paul Strebel of the State University of New York at Binghamton, we found that at any given time in the last ten years, almost one third of the companies included in the Standard and Poor's 500 index received little regular coverage of any substance. Of course, a much larger percentage of neglected companies can be found outside the popular fraternity of the S&P 500. Thus, when you consider the whole investment opportunity set, including stocks listed on the American Stock Exchange and the Over-the-Counter market, the number of neglected stocks at any particular time reaches thousands of stocks.

A question immediately relating to this definition of neglect is, Don't analysts shift their attention quite frequently?

Of course they do. This has to be taken into consideration in any attempt to evaluate the past performance of neglected stocks and to apply the Neglected Firm Effect as a practical investment strategy. This shift in analysts' attention is called the *popularity flow* and it is a key component in applying the Generic Stock Investment Strategy, but this important point will be discussed later. First let's finish with the definitions.

Degree of neglect can also be measured in another way, that is, by actual investor behavior, as observed in the market. According to this approach, a stock is neglected if it is not widely held by financial institutions, i.e., by the big money guys. Institutional investors include, among others, investment companies, mutual funds, trusts, pension funds, banks, insurance companies, not-for-profit foundations, and other large investors.

Neglect in this context means, in fact, *institutional neglect*. The orphans are those who don't have any "big daddies."

Several research studies, including our own, have found a high degree of overlap between the two measures of neglect. This is not surprising, because if financial institutions are avoiding certain stocks (usually, but not only of smaller companies), financial analysts tend to avoid them as well. Also, though to a lesser degree, this relationship exists in reverse. In either case, information vacuums prevail. This is the area where neglected stocks flourish.

It was found that the superior market performance of neglected stocks occurs when neglect is defined by either of the two measures. That is, lack of institutional attention and lack of analyst attention are both highly correlated with superior market performance.

The fact that these two measures can largely substitute for each other is important from the practical point of view. Current data on institutional holdings, and therefore, by elimination, on institutional nonholdings, are easy to get, making this contrariant investment approach likewise easy to implement.

In considering measures of neglect, the dynamics of the process should not be ignored. In many cases the *change* in the level of analyst attention or institutional holding might be as important a yardstick as the absolute measure. Remember, we are talking about a process; we are concerned with the dynamics of the information dissemination process. In this respect, the incremental effect is important—this is what determines prices in any economic process (e.g., *changes* in interest rates are often more important in affecting demand for housing than the absolute numbers). Later on we shall discuss the fascinating case of Chrysler Corporation in which the decline (i.e., change) in its popularity among institutional investors made it one of the best investments in 1982.

This suggests that a relative measure of neglect is important not only among all companies but also for the same company over time. A decline in the level of attention for a highly followed stock is an important signal that should be considered.

Other Measures of Neglect

While the two measures of neglect discussed above seem to best identify neglected stocks, other measures can also be considered. These measures are more problematic; therefore they should be used as supplementary measures only.

It has been suggested that the stock's average daily volume of trading might be a useful indication of investors' interest in a stock, for example, that low volume implies neglect. However, one has to be careful with the volume measure because it is biased by a company's size. For example, a volume of five thousand shares per day is considered low for IBM but might represent an extremely high level of interest in some very small company with a small number of shares outstanding. Also, you have to adjust for the overall volume of trade for the market on a given day. Therefore, it is necessary to consider *relative* volume, that is, the number of shares traded as a percentage of the total outstanding shares of the company in relation to the market volume as a whole. This is more complicated than the two measures of neglect previously discussed.

One can think of several other measures of neglect, such as low price/earnings (P/E) ratio, low dollar share price, small number of shares outstanding or small market capitalization, etc. While all these can be used as supplementary measures, it cannot be overemphasized that as far as understanding the Neglected Firm Effect, and attempting to use this phenomenon toward an effective investment strategy, are concerned, it is important to select measures of neglect or popularity, that have direct or indirect *informational content*. Remember that the whole idea of degree of neglect relates to the availability and quality of information. The two measures just described before, namely, number of analysts who follow the stock and number of institutions holding the stock, are the best indexes of degree of neglect. Both reflect the informational content (quantity, quality, availability), the former in a more direct way and the latter by implication.

What about relative volume and the other measures? These are less direct, less explicit, and therefore they tend to reveal less about the Neglected Firm Effect than do the more direct measures. Empirical evidence discussed later shows that this is the case.

Food for Thought 1: The Meat Slicers, the Mail Orders, and You

Consider how life could have been different for you today if in 1914 you had bought 100 shares of an obscure little company that produced meat slicers, scales for grocery stores, time clocks, and some strange new things called tabulators promoted shamelessly as "business machines." The 100 shares of this company would have cost you (okay, perhaps not you, but your grandfather) $27.50 a share, or a total of $2,750, plus commission. This company, called IBM wandered for many years in the shadows and then turned out to be the growth company of the century. As a result of several good splits over the years, your original 100 shares would have grown to 291,192 shares with a market value of over $35 million in 1984. This figure does not include a very substantial dividend income that IBM has paid every year since 1916.

I personally know some retired employees of IBM living in a small, somewhat neglected town in upstate New York called Endicott—where IBM started. In the early days they got hundreds of shares as a portion of their pay. They and others who believed in the company also bought shares practically for nothing. They are multimillionaires today. You don't need a P.C. to figure it out.

Or, your grandfather could have done the same with a small unknown mail-order house in 1906; he could have bought 100 shares for about $5,000. The initial investment would have been worth more than $24.5 million in 1984 (excluding dividends). You may have guessed: The mail-order company is Sears, Roebuck.

More recently, in 1980–81, the old, tired ugly duckling Chrysler Corporation that everybody deserted just before it turned beautiful; the best investment in 1982 among all stocks listed on the big board.

Or, you may want to consider investing tomorrow in Yatom Corporation. Yatom Corporation is a small new company located in California, probably hidden in some deep valley. It might have recently invented a chemical chicken soup that among other things cures herpes, baldness, and unwanted pregnancy. The company, so the rumors say, has several patents but has not yet received approval from the FDA or even the EPA. I'll bet that your broker never heard of it. It is still highly neglected, but not for long. . . . So if you can, go find it and become rich!

The Neglected Firm Effect
as a Testable Hypothesis—
Some of the Background

Whatever the best definition of neglect is, the notion that neglected stocks are likely to perform better is not a new one among practitioners. "What else is new?" was the blasé response of some old market wolves when I enthusiastically presented them with a fresh crop of research findings, just out of the fanciest computerized modeling system that I could design, regarding the superb performance of neglected stocks. In fact, it is such an intuitively appealing idea that once you think about it, it is hard to reject. It simply makes sense. However, there is a difference between market legends and a proven hypothesis rigorously tested and found to be not only supported statistically but also consistent with some logical theory or accepted model. In this sense the Neglected Firm Effect is a brand-new theorem—and so is its practical offshoot, the Generic Stock Investment Strategy.

The concept of the Neglected Firm Effect is only now emerging out of the rigorous, seemingly endless, and somewhat painful testing process. For a long time it has been shaping up and stewing in the usual social science lab, in the finance departments of universities, slowly moving through the tortuous screening process. First, academics somehow develop the theory. Then they test it in those cold, fluorescent-lit cement basements where computer terminals usually are located. Huge data bases are compiled, checked, cleaned, and duplicated; Ph.D. dissertations are written and rewritten; and simultaneously, working papers shyly appear. Results are first presented in internal "faculty and advanced student seminars" where the debate, usually among the professors themselves, goes on and on forever. At almost the same time, the better research results, packaged now as "research papers," are presented in academic and professional conferences. Then, if they survive, they move on. Clean, well-organized articles with all the academic trimmings of elegant equations, graphs, sexy models, and a lot of overly sophisticated terminology are written, submitted for publication, rejected, rewritten, and finally published. And some, if lucky, even win academic prizes.

Practitioners closely follow this process, always anxious to be the first to pick up some new "workable" investment strategy to improve market performance of their stocks. The ever-present, efficient financial journalists and publicity-minded professors help in this respect. For example:

Gary Putka, a highly respected journalist from *The Wall Street Journal* wrote in his column, "Heard on the Street," on April 7, 1983:

> Some academic studies say that the less a company is followed by Wall Street, the better its stock-market performance. In keeping with this thinking, Mr. Kildoyle says his ideal stock is one without any analyst coverage at all, which is trading at about two times its peak earnings, and has a market value well below its book value.

Somewhat jokingly, Mr. Putka continues:

> Mr. Kildoyle, who was tracked down yesterday in a hotel room in Sydney, Australia—presumably a good place to look for companies Wall Street is missing . . .

Mr. Putka then goes on to discuss some specific investment ideas in the area of neglected stocks.

In a somewhat more direct reference, Mr. Putka writes in his June 3, 1982, *Wall Street Journal* column:

> According to a new investment study on stock picking . . . a wide following by analysts may by itself guarantee mediocre market performance for a given stock.
>
> The study, entitled "The Neglected and Small Firm Effects," recently won an award for the best research presented at a conference of the Eastern Finance Association, a large organization of finance professors. It is also scheduled to be published in the summer issue of The Financial Review, an academic quarterly. Study authors Avner Arbel and Paul Strebel, of the State University of New York at Binghamton, found that an investment strategy based on picking only those stocks with light analyst coverage would have yielded superior returns in the market in the 1970's.
>
> Stocks in the Standard & Poor's 500 with one analyst, or none, following them, turned in a total return for the period of 16% a year, according to the paper.

The article continues to describe the study results in more detail, and then presenting some controversy (even the serious readers of *The Wall Street Journal* like to see some blood), it says:

> The study may shake up some investment theoreticians, as it tends to cast doubt on the popular "efficient market theory" which holds that no one can beat the market averages consistently. The findings also suggest something that may be unsettling to many on Wall Street: that the biggest gains on a stock may already be behind it before brokerage house analysts begin following it.

The article goes on to describe how another study done by a highly qualified practitioner, Salomon Brothers, clearly confirms the professors' results. Then the professors briefly present their opinion about the whys and the how-to and, of course, respond to the unavoidable question, What neglected issues with good prospects fill Mr. Arbel's portfolio?

When such blessed publicity occurs in what is claimed to be the most widely read financial column in the Western world, the research process continues more smoothly. Suddenly everybody is interested; it is easier to raise funds for further academic research, and new computer tapes are filled with surprisingly important data from resourceful, previously hidden sources who suddenly are interested in helping you with your research. It is also now easier to attract better graduate students to work with you. As a result, more and better research follows—supported by a lot of feedback from researchers in other universities all over the world, and most importantly, from practitioners who rush to test the latest research results with new investment strategies.

The more popular news media is now attracted. For example, the following appeared on the national *CBS Morning News* on June 27, 1983:

> *Ken Prewitt:*   A recent study covering ten years of stock market activity by Professor Avner Arbel at Cornell University says the kind of stocks to buy are the ones the institutions don't want. The Arbel study says the brand-name stocks, the ones with heavy institutional ownership have returned an average of ten percent a year, not bad, but the generic stocks, the ones the institutions don't want, have returned twenty-one percent. Arbel says there is a catch, the generic stocks are

not widely followed, so you have to do your
homework.

Diane Sawyer: Thank you, Ken. Here's some brand-
name weather—Steve Dasler.

Steve Dasler: Boy, no sooner do you finish school and
there's more homework. . . .

And in *Money* magazine (December 1983):

Individual investors do not have to worry about caus-
ing market turbulence or justifying their stock picks to a
fickle clientele. They go prospecting in a less efficient
market of 6,000 or so stocks that most of the institutions
ignore and few, if any analysts bother with. Recent his-
tory suggests that those are the shares that, as a class,
produce the biggest profits. . . .

Scouring the Underbrush
Cornell professor Avner Arbel compares institutional
investors to "giraffes that nibble on the tall trees in the
investment forest and ignore the underbrush." Since he
believes that the biggest potential winners lie hidden in
that underbrush, he strongly favors stocks owned by
fewer than five institutional investors. You can find out
how many institutions hold a stock by looking it up in
Standard & Poor's Stock Guide, which all brokers and
many libraries have.

Sounds easy. Unfortunately a bit more is involved here.
The road to wealth and happiness is a trifle longer and
the process is somewhat more involved. Seriously, you
don't really expect to hitchhike all the way to the sev-
enth heaven.

But is the effort worthwhile? Let's look at the evidence.

Some Hard Evidence on Market Performance of Neglected Stocks

Consider the following performance measures of neglected stocks.

Table 1 presents actual returns—capital gains (or losses) plus dividends—for a period of ten years for all stocks included in the S&P 500 index. These stocks are separated into three subcatagories according to the level of attention given to each stock by security analysts. The annual returns for the most highly followed stocks are presented in column 1, while the returns for the most neglected stocks are presented in column 3. What do those figures tell us?

First, the average annual returns, including dividends, for the most neglected stocks are considerably higher than for the more highly followed companies: 16 percent versus 9 percent. This is quite a difference—and please note, these results refer to *all* 500 stocks in the Standard and Poor's index; there was no screening to distinguish among companies of different financial strengths or business potentials. The only selection criterion used was degree of neglect. You can imagine how the performance of neglected stocks can be improved by implementing even a very basic screening. We will return to this important point later in the next how-to chapter.

TABLE 1   Average Annual Return by Degree of Neglect 1970–1979 (in %)*

	1. Highly Followed Stocks	2. Moderately Followed Stocks	3. Neglected Stocks
1970	2.7	4.6	7.0
1971	20.5	24.7	16.5
1972	15.3	16.0	16.8
1973	−15.6	−18.9	−8.9
1974	−23.7	−24.6	−11.8
1975	46.5	58.1	60.8
1976	22.0	35.7	43.9
1977	−.56	−.01	2.8
1978	7.7	6.6	8.5
1979	24.3	25.2	28.0
Average† per Year 1970–1979	9.4	12.7	16.4

*Including dividend
†Simple arithmetic average
Source: A. Arbel and P. J. Strebel, "Pay Attention to Neglected Firms!," *Journal of Portfolio Management* (Winter 1983), pp. 37–42.

Second, the data clearly shows that the Neglected Firm Effect, in terms of better performance, has persisted through every year of the decade except 1971. Thus, it seems that we have here a continuous and consistent phenomenon.

Third, you might ask, What about risk? Clearly, one cannot evaluate return without considering risk because, as a rule, the two go together; the higher the risk the higher the expected return over the long run. Neglected companies might have more volatility in prices and returns, and therefore they might be more risky. Or they might be more volatile in relation to the market as a whole. In both cases the higher return might be a just reward (and perhaps even an insufficient one) for sleepless nights.

In order to cope satisfactorily with the risk factor, some basic theoretical tools are required at this point. They will also be helpful for the rest of the discussion presented in this book.

Risk theory is one of those aspects of finance that is still somewhat sticky and difficult to grasp. It is much easier to experience risk than to understand it. But let's get it over with and try to cope with the basics of risk theory as soon as possible. And remember that time and again throughout this book explanations of the somewhat difficult concepts of risk measures will be repeated in different ways to ensure that even if you miss some of it now you'll still have another chance later.

Traditionally, risk is measured in terms of return volatility. The more fluctuations there are in a stock's price and dividend, the higher is the risk. According to modern investment theory, two types of risk can be distinguished: systematic and unsystematic. Systematic risk is market-related risk. This is the part of the variability in stock return that is related to fluctuations in the market performance as a whole. Take IBM as an example. When its price moves up and down over time, part of these fluctuations are related to the market as a whole, or the economy. Thus, when there is a recession IBM suffers like most other companies and likewise in good times it gains. When the market goes substantially down, practically all stocks go down, and the opposite occurs when the market moves up. Virtually all stocks are affected by this market-related risk, though in differing intensities. Because of this tendency for stocks to move together, this type of risk is called *systematic*. It is almost impossible to get rid of this risk by diversification.

When everything moves virtually in the same direction, you don't have the offsetting effect so critical for risk reduction by diversification. The systematic risk is usually measured by the "beta coefficient," which is an index of a stock's systematic risk; the larger the beta, the higher is the systematic risk, or the more volatile is the stock vis-à-vis the market as a whole.

The other type of risk is called *unsystematic* risk. This is the component of a stock's total return volatility, which is related to the performance of the company itself or the relevant industry. Consider IBM again. Part of its price volatility relates to how successful IBM is as a company, and how investors perceive its future potential and risk compared with that of all other companies in the industry and in other industries. Since each company has its own unsystematic risk characteristics, which are related to other companies' risk in a different way, it is possible to reduce or sometimes even to eliminate this risk by correct diversification. In fact, a well-diversified portfolio will have only systematic (market-related) risk, while the unsystematic risk will be diversified away. An extreme case of complete diversification is, of course, the market portfolio. This is a portfolio that contains all available stocks. It will not have any unsystematic (company-related) risk at all, but only the market risk; the rest will be completely diversified away. (An easy logical proof: the market portfolio by definition will encounter the volatility of the market as a whole, nothing below or above it. Therefore total risk in this case is just the market risk). We shall come back to this point when the idea of diversification is introduced as a key element of the generic stock investment approach.

In summary, total risk is measured in terms of volatility. Volatility can be separated into systematic or market-related volatility, as measured by the beta, and unsystematic or overall company-related volatility. The latter can be eliminated, or at least reduced, in a well-diversified portfolio. The former is a necessary evil, invented no doubt by the devil himself, which one must live with.

How do our sleeping beauties, the neglected stocks, compare in this respect to the market as a whole? Do they have a higher level of systematic risk? In other words, are their prices more volatile than the market as a whole? And, given that many investors are not fully diversified, what about the company-related risk, the unsystematic risk?

Our research revealed only minor differences in the observed systematic risk, or market-related risk, as measured in the usual way by the beta coefficient, between stocks of different degrees of neglect. Also, the unsystematic risk does not greatly change with degree of neglect. Evidently, the regular measures of risk, most widely used by academics as well as practitioners, were unable to detect a higher level of risk associated with neglected stocks. As a result, the risk-adjusted returns for stocks of different neglect rankings exhibited a pattern similar to that of the unadjusted returns. Neglected stocks perform much better even after the usual adjustment for risk.

The evidence regarding risk-adjusted returns is presented in Table 2.

What counts, of course, are the risk-adjusted measures, and here they are bright and clear.*

*Readers who are interested in a more theoretical and somewhat technical discussion on the relative performance of neglected stocks are referred to an article, "The Neglected and Small Firm Effects," by Professor Paul J. Strebel and Avner Arbel in the *Financial Review*, vol. 17, no. 4 (November 1982). Other references in which different measures of neglect have been used will be presented later.

**TABLE 2   Average Annual Return and Risk-Adjusted
Return by Degree of Neglect 1970–1979***

	Unadjusted	Risk-Adjusted Return†		
	Averaged Annual Return (%)	Excess Return (%)	Return per Unit of Unsystematic Risk	Return per Unit of Total Risk
1. Highly Followed	9.4	−2.6	.384	.276
2. Moderate	12.7	.5	.525	.353
3. Neglected	16.4	3.7	.669	.443

*Return includes dividend; averages are unweighted.

†Excess returns were calculated based on the Capital Asset Pricing Model. Conceptually, these returns represent abnormal returns over and above what is justified by the risk adjustment used by the model. For further explanation see page 158. The key point is that higher abnormal returns were found for neglected stocks over and above the risk premium justified by the model. Return per unit of unsystematic risk and of total risk (the last two columns) are simply the appropriate returns divided by the relevant measures of volatility (risk).

Source: A. Arbel and P. J. Strebel, "Pay Attention to Neglected Firms!," *Journal of Portfolio Management* (Winter 1983), p. 37.

Table 2 shows that differences in systematic risk cannot explain the Neglected Firm Effect. Neither can differences in unsystematic risk. The second column clearly indicates that returns adjusted for the systematic (market-related) risk substantially increase with degree of neglect. The third column shows that the same is true for unsystematic (company-related) risk; again the risk-adjusted return rises markedly with the degree of neglect. The message seems clear: even if we accept the (realistic) assumption that many investors do not completely diversify and therefore unsystematic risk still counts, neglected companies greatly outperformed the more popular companies.

The results for returns adjusted for total risk, which

is the sum of the systematic and unsystematic risk, are now expected. Look at the last column of Table 2. It summarizes the risk adjustment story as a whole. Differences in the traditional measures of total risk cannot explain the better performance of neglected stocks. Amazingly, the return of the most neglected stocks was more than 60 percent higher than for the most followed stocks even after adjustment for total risk! So, maybe Cinderellas do exist?

Note that we have repeatedly used the terms "usual" or "traditional" in referring to measures of risk. Keep this in mind. Risk might have other dimensions not captured by the usual measures. We shall return to this key point later.

Relative Performance of Neglected Stocks According to Other Measures of Neglect

Does the superior market performance of neglected stocks also prevail when neglect is measured in terms of the second measure discussed above, namely, lack of institutional attention? Yes, very much so. In a recent article published in the *Financial Analysts Journal,* it has been shown that institutionally neglected stocks, as a group, perform much better than the institutions' favorite stocks. The findings described in the article are summarized in Table 3.

In this study, we followed a straightforward approach to assessing stocks. First, a large number of stocks were selected at random and in equal quantities from the three stock exchanges: the New York, the American, and the Over-the-Counter. These stocks have been classified into three groups according to their level of institutional holding. We thus had three portfolios of stocks: (a) stocks most favored by financial institutions, (b) the most neglected stocks, and (c) those in between. Then, for each of the three portfolios, returns and several measures of

TABLE 3   Stocks' Average Annual Returns, Risk Measures and Risk-Adjusted Returns by Level of Institutional Holdings 1971–1980

Level of Institutional Holding	Returns* (%)	Risk		Risk-Adjusted Returns		
		Total	Systematic	Excess Return†	Sharpe Index‡	Treynor Index‡
Intensively Held	10.4 (.028)	.337	.99	−.0580	.12	.040
Moderately Held	16.9 (.036)	.428	.92	.0111	.25	.114
Institutionally Neglected	20.8 (.034)	.536	.90	.0564	.27	.160

*Standard errors of estimates are given in parenthesis.

†Based on the Capital Asset Pricing Model. See footnote 2 in Table 2.

‡The Sharpe Index basically measures return over and above the prevailing riskless rate, per unit of total risk. While the Treynor Index measures the same return per unit of systematic (market-related) risk. The numbers simply represent reward for risk taking. Other things being equal, the larger the number the better.

Source: A. Arbel, S. Carvell, and P. J. Strebel, "Giraffes, Institutions and Neglected Firms," *Financial Analysts Journal* (May/June 1983), pp. 60–69.

risk were calculated for every year and averaged for the entire period of ten years. Also, risk-adjusted returns were calculated and compared. What were the results?

First, the data clearly indicates that market segmentation does exist: about one third of the companies in our random cross-market sample were neglected by financial institutions, that is, were held by no financial institution at all or by just one.

Second, a highly significant Neglected Firm Effect exists. Returns rise sharply as institutional holding declines. In fact, for the 1970–80 decade, the average annual returns for the institutionally neglected securities were twice the returns for stocks most widely held by financial institutions, by a pretty impressive 20.8 percent compared with 10.4 percent.

What about risk? Even when adjusted for the usual measures of risk, the Neglected Firm Effect again comes through strong and clear: On the average, the neglected portfolios earned more than double the return per unit of risk than the widely held portfolios, and even four times as much, depending on whether the risk adjustment was done with total risk (Sharpe Index) or with beta (Treynor Index).* The same results are apparent when excess returns, as measured according to the Capital Asset Pricing Model,† are used. The widely held institutional sweetheart portfolio had an average annual excess return of 8.6 percent below the market, while the neglected portfolio was 5.8 percent above the market.

The theme of our study of institutional holding is that the Neglected Firm Effect was confirmed even when we used a different and, as we shall see soon, a more read-

*See short explanations for these indexes in footnote 3 to Table 3.

†See the short explanation in footnote 2, Table 2, and a more detailed discussion on page 158, where the reasons for the Neglected Firm Effect are given.

ily available, ex post measure of neglect. Also, for this study we used a broader sample and somewhat different and more robust research techniques, and arrived at the same conclusion: The orphans eventually thrive and the wallflowers turn beautiful.

Size or Neglect — What Does Really Matter?

There is an interesting and relevant point that has been creating some confusion in the financial literature, which I want to discuss next. It relates to the relationship between company size and its degree of neglect. Or, put in different terms, the relationship between the Small Firm Effect and the Neglected Firm Effect. Recall that several researchers, practitioners, and academics have found that small firms consistently outperform large firms in overall market return. (See for example the data presented in Table 4.) If indeed small firms perform better in the market, is it not possible that the Neglected Firm Effect is a mere reflection of company size?

The evidence does not support this notion. On the contrary, there are reasons to believe that size is just a surrogate for something else, that the excess return of small firms is a reflection of a factor that is related to size, but is not a factor of size itself. After all, what's so special about being small? Why should company size, as such, affect the pricing mechanism and reward higher

TABLE 4 Market Performance: Small Versus Large Companies

Average Annual Compound Returns for Five-Year Periods (1933–1982). (Stock group performances have been adjusted to account for varying risk factors.)

	Small Stocks	S&P 500
1933–1937	35.5	14.3
1938–1942	5.2	4.6
1943–1947	37.8	14.8
1948–1952	13.6	19.4
1953–1957	11.0	13.6
1958–1962	17.3	13.3
1963–1967	30.2	12.4
1968–1972	3.5	7.5
1973–1977	8.2	−0.2
1978–1982	28.7	14.0

Source: Diversified Financial Advisors, published in *The New York Times,* December 11, 1983.

return? If this higher return is not a compensation for something (that deserves higher return), how can it survive over time (and not be grabbed by greedy investors as a free gift and consequently disappear)? And, the key question: What is that something that deserves, and indeed generates, the observed higher return? No doubt, there must be more to it than just smallness itself.

As will be shown in the last, more theoretical, part of this book, this higher return can be explained and, in fact, its absence cannot be justified once the idea of generic stock is incorporated. We shall see that there exists here information deficiency premium rather than size premium.

What is the evidence about the relationship between size and neglect as found in some of our recent studies?

1. The outstanding performance of small firms' stocks does not prevail once returns are correctly adjusted for *total* risk. Small firms do have higher returns but their returns are also more volatile.

2. When controlled for degree of neglect (either as defined by analyst attention or by institutional holding) the Small Firm Effect largely disappears. That is, the performance of small popular firms is not better than the performance of large popular firms. Also, large neglected companies perform better than small popular companies.

3. Our findings point to a possible reverse small firm effect: Among the more institutionally popular securities the larger firms (and not the smaller) perform better.

In summary, firms neglected by institutions and/or by analysts outperformed the popular ones, on a risk-adjusted basis, even after correcting for size. Several methods of correcting for size were used but the results persist: neglect and not size seems to be the underlying cause of the outstanding performance. It is true, however, that size is clearly highly related to neglect. But this correlation is less than perfect. It means that the orphans are usually small, but not always. The main point is that the orphans as a group are bound to be eventually successful not because they are small but because they are still to be discovered. It is information rather than size that matters.

Food for Thought 2: Market Efficiency and the Zambatoto Stock Exchange

You may have heard about the market efficiency hypothesis, so widely acclaimed. It asserts that the stock market is efficient in the sense that at any given time all relevant information is immediately and fully reflected in stock prices. Therefore, no underpriced (or overpriced) stocks can be found in the market, no bargains, and it's impossible to beat the market. You get what you pay for (in risk/return terms). Financial assets are fairly priced.

The "random walk" notion takes things even one step further. It claims that stock prices fluctuate in a random way.

So, by using darts to select stocks, these theories would have you believe, you'll be as effective as with any other approach. Definitely don't use technical analysis, and don't even bother to do fundamental analysis. It's too late, anyhow. Don't call your broker for advice; it's a waste of time and money. Furthermore, the efficient market hypothesis has profit implications. It tells you to reduce your expectations, that over the long run you will not make above-average return, which is the appropriate reward for the level of risk taken. Nothing more.

Don't shop around, just buy—in accordance with the level of risk that you are willing to take. And, of course, diversify a lot to reduce risk. Buy at random and diversify. Don't try to beat and you won't be beaten. This is the message of the market efficiency breed. Not a very encouraging message.

Fine. But what if some segments of the market are not as efficient as others? What if some stocks suffer from information deficiency because, for some good reasons, they are neglected by most financial institutions and consequently are not widely followed?

In this gray segment of the market, shouldn't one expect a slower adjustment process to new information? and, therefore, for a while, some underpriced and overpriced stocks?

Isn't the notion of information efficiency indeed the key prerequisite for market efficiency? And is it realistic to assume that all stocks are at all times identical in this respect?

Imagine the Zambatoto Stock Exchange. Zambatoto is a small emerging country located someplace. There is hardly one newspaper over there. The telephone system is battered and unreliable. They do have a radio station but it broadcasts only local music for a full four hours daily (more or less, depending on the availability of electricity). The government and the system as a whole require very little public disclosure. There is practically no information, and people react slowly because of the heat and for other reasons. The big money guys are not active over there. They simply don't exist. There are some industries in the state of Zambatoto and the Zambatotians are greedy like the rest of us. So, they have a stock exchange.

—Would you expect market efficiency in the Zambatoto Stock Exchange?

—Would it be reasonable to assume that many American neglected stocks live in Zambatoto?

Two Amazing Market Phenomena: The January and the Low P/E Puzzles

Amazingly, the Small Firm Effect and the Neglected Firm Effect are not the end of the story known as *market anomalies*. These are only the tip of the iceberg. Let me add some others: It was found, checked, and reconfirmed by some of the brightest minds in financial research that most of the outstanding performance of small firms occurs in January of every year. In fact, mainly in just a few days at the turn of the year. Again, this phenomenon, dubbed the January Effect, has persisted in almost every year for the last twenty years—which is the limit of the detailed data available that is required to rigorously check it.

Why these high returns in January? Why mainly small firms? How can it persist over time? And the most irritating question: Why can't the existing theory cope with this phenomenon and explain it? In fact, the January Effect recently caused so much confusion that one of the most highly regarded professors and researchers in fi-

nance, Professor Richard Roll of UCLA, published an
article about it in the *Journal of Portfolio Management*
(Winter 1983) entitled "Vas Ist Das?"

And that isn't all. For many years researchers and
practitioners have been astonished by what is now called
the Low P/E Anomaly. In this case, stocks with low
price/earnings ratios as a group consistently and substantially outperformed stocks of a higher P/E. Again the
same questions can be asked: why? and how can it persist? and all the rest.

These questions are difficult to answer. They not only
present an intellectual challenge but they also have far-
reaching profit implications.

You probably sense by now that the four anomalies—
the Small Firm Effect, the Neglected Firm Effect, the
Low P/E Anomaly, and the January Effect—must somehow be related. Logic also tells you that the persisting
higher returns in all these cases cannot be a free gift. After
all, Wall Street is quite far from the promised land and
even up there they don't have open enrollment. These
excess returns must represent reward for something. In
other words, they have to be earned. But reward for
what?

I propose that they are all related to a common informational variable that affects investors' perceived risk
level. They all represent surrogates of what will be called
generic premium—a premium that is well deserved and
can be earned. Keep this point in mind. The whys and
the how-to will be explained in the following pages.

The Market Price Leaders— Who Are They?

At any given time, one can identify some stocks that outperform all the rest. They are called the market leaders. In retrospect one can jealously observe such leaders for every day, week, month, quarter, year, or if you wish, for the last decade. This is true by definition—some stocks do better than others. However, the interesting point is that as a rule, regardless of the period considered—from one day to a full ten-year period or more—this outstanding group of fliers outperformed the typical stock by several orders of magnitude. In simple terms, this means that for any given period of time you have some super winners that, for whatever reasons, produce extremely high capital gains. The leaders are way ahead of the rest of the crowd. In fact, it is not abnormal to find stocks with *daily* returns of 25 percent or more, which is the equivalent of a 6,500 percent annualized return. (Are you surprised? Check the small "Daily Percentage" table published daily at the page next to the last of *The Wall Street Journal*.)

Obviously, every investor would like to have as many of those leaders in his or her portfolio as possible.

In an effort to serve such investors, and not ignoring our own desires, we, a team of market researchers, have asked ourselves the obvious, somewhat naïve question: What is the common denominator of the leaders? and the immediate follow-up question: How can one identify the leaders in advance?

In fact, we tried to model mathematically the idea of producing tomorrow's *Wall Street Journal* today by studying the leaders and the distinct characteristics of the jumps. We used hours of computer time, a brigade of graduate assistants, and every relevant statistical computer package that we could find. We tried everything: simulations, regression analysis, discriminate analysis, factor analysis, cluster analysis, the relatively new nonparametric "neighbor" procedure, as well as some of the more established techniques like the Gutman Approach.

What did we find?

Nothing! Or, to be more precise, nothing in terms of the usual variables that are believed to generate abnormal returns such as distinct industry group, concept groups (e.g., high tech), reaction to occurrence or announcement of specific events like unexpected higher earnings, dividends, splits, new products, or mergers. Of course, these events create sporadic short-term large jumps in prices. But only sometimes. Evidently, these variables and many others that we tried cannot predict a leader. None is a consistent common denominator for most of the really big jumps. We have found that many big daily jumps occur without any detectable event prior to the jump.

This in fact confirms previous research. The literature is full of studies showing that many events like the ones just mentioned, once publicly announced, are not followed by immediate price jumps. Thus, it seems that there is no consistent, statistically significant common denominator for the spectacular market leaders. That is, except one: or maybe I should say at this point, *the* one.

The orphans are jumping, the orphans are jumping. You might have guessed.

Yes, indeed they are, and remarkably high! We found that as a rule most, though (please note) not all, of the leaders are neglected stocks. In fact, we found that this is the only detectable partial common denominator. It relates to either definition of neglect, or both: namely, analyst following and/or institutional holding. Furthermore, and perhaps as conspicuous, this conclusion applies not only to the daily market leaders but also to the top performers of any other time span; weekly, monthly, quarterly, and annually.

What about size? Aren't the leaders also mostly small companies? the skeptic in you might ask, still not forgetting about the Small Firm Effect.

Yes, this is true, but neglect is again the underlying factor, not size. For example, many large but relatively neglected companies can often be found on the leaders list but hardly any small and highly followed companies.

A fascinating example of this is Chrysler Corporation in 1982.

The tired, old (and big!) Chrysler Corporation, half dead and most neglected, in fact almost despised by both financial institutions and analysts, outperformed all other companies in 1982; its return for the year was 426 percent.

Recall that I have mentioned the measure of *change* in popularity as an important indicator for degree of neglect. Indeed, the number of financial institutions holding Chrysler stock dropped from many hundreds in the late sixties to 85 in May 1977 and later to a mere 29 in December 1981, compared with, for example, 532 institutions investing in IBM. This is a typical case of a company that had suffered from popularity slide, or investors' overreaction.

A very similar example is New York City bonds in

1976–77. Many investors doubled their money, and with bonds, mind you, not stocks! They made a fortune by investing in the Big Apple, which turned out to be not as sour as previously perceived by most financial institutions and analysts. Here again neglect and not size was the key factor.

The performance of the Apple Computer Corporation is an example of market success of an emerging company that followed the growth of the company. In May 1980 the company was so neglected that it was not even listed in the *Standard & Poor's Stock Guide*. When it finally appeared in December 1980, not even one financial institution held Apple Computer stocks, according to the S&P reports. Check it today. Institutions are prudently married to the company now and the party is over: no more huge jumps in prices. Change the time frame of the fairy tale and the same Cinderella story can be told about Xerox, IBM, McDonald's, Disney, and many other now classic success stories. This suggests that maybe Mr. Bernard Baruch was right in saying, as the legend goes, that one should buy when there is blood in the streets.

Or, perhaps the rule should be, Buy straw hats in December when everybody else is buying fur coats. This is the essence of the neglected stock investment idea. Though, let's not kid ourselves, buying a straw hat is much simpler than successfully investing in stocks.

We have just seen some extreme examples of neglected leaders' performance. Let's now look at more systematic data: an analysis, done at Cornell University, based on a representative sample of the most outstanding daily price leaders, which outperformed all other stocks in 1981 and 1982. The study reveals that approximately 90 percent of the top price leaders were completely neglected by analysts, that is, were followed by only one major analyst or no analyst at all, on a continual basis at the time just before the big jump. About 5 percent were followed by two to four analysts; only 5 percent were somewhat popular with analysts. Similar conclusions apply to the institutional holding measure of neglect.

Interestingly, and not at all surprisingly, even within this group that was pretty homogeneous in terms of its lack of popularity, a statistically significant pattern can be observed: as a rule, the more neglected the stock is, the higher the jump in returns. Thus, even within the neglected group the most highly neglected stocks tend to jump more.

To demonstrate this point, take for example a more recent set of data, for the stocks that outperformed all others in the first quarter of 1983, as published in the April 4, 1983, issue of *The Wall Street Journal* (see Table 5).

As you can see not even one company among the top leaders was listed on the more widely followed New York Stock Exchange (six were on the American and four

TABLE 5   Stock Market Performance—10 Biggest Gainers: First Quarter 1983

Company	Stock Exchange	No. of Institutions Holding the Stock (Dec. 1982)	% Change in Price
Dentomed Ind.	O.T.C.	0	700
Acme Precision	American	0	311
Amer. Magnetics	O.T.C.	0	233
Electro Catheter	O.T.C.	0	229
Rowe Furniture	O.T.C.	4	229
Casablanca Inds.	American	0	224
Technicom Intl.	American	7	157
Lloyds Electronics	American	0	153
Andrea Radio	American	0	135
Kleer VU Inds.	American	1	131

Source: The Wall Street Journal, April 4, 1983. Data on institutions' holdings were taken from the *Standard & Poor's Stock Guide,* December 1982.

Over-the-Counter). All the price leaders were virtually neglected by financial institutions. Even the most highly followed stock among this group of top winners, Technicom International, was held by just seven financial institutions.

Let's look at the other extreme—the real lemons. Table 6 presents the data for the ten biggest losers for the same period.

Just compare the measures of neglect and performance for the losers and the gainers (the last two columns in Table 5 and 6) and the point will be clear. The darlings seem to be heading south!

Pick at random *The Wall Street Journal* of any day. Check the list of the "Daily Percentage" leaders (usually appearing on the next-to-last page of the second section). Count how many of the top leaders are small, unknown, low-price companies and how many are well-known highly followed companies. Repeat the experi-

TABLE 6   Stock Market Performance—10 Biggest Losers: First Quarter 1983

Company	Stock Exchange	No. of Institutions Holding the Stock (Dec. 1982)	% Change in Price
Baldwin-Utd.	N.Y.S.E.	58	−63
Veta Grande	O.T.C.	1	−51
Wesper Corp.	American	3	−51
A. T. Bliss	O.T.C.	0	−50
Galveston Houston	N.Y.S.E.	29	−39
Nutri Systems	N.Y.S.E.	23	−37
Orrox	American	1	−36
Mitel	N.Y.S.E.	93	−33
Page Peter	American	16	−32
Mattel	N.Y.S.E.	100	−32

Source: The Wall Street Journal, April 4, 1983.

ment for several more days. Do the same for longer time spans—weeks, months, years, or longer. What's your conclusion?

An Intermediate Summary

So far we have seen some definitions and a lot of evidence. It might be appropriate now to pause for a moment for a short summary.

The evidence shows that not only have neglected stocks consistently outperformed the more closely followed stocks over the years, and on a risk-adjusted basis, but that neglected securities exhibit by far the largest price jumps. Among the market's biggest front-runners, neglected stocks always dominate. The analysis of the leaders presented above, together with the evidence on the big jump of neglected stocks in January (see discussion on the January Effect coming soon) and some other evidence, suggest that in general neglected stocks move in jumps and follow a less gradual path than the more popular brand-name stocks. Evidently, they react to some shocks which, as will be explained in the last part of this book, are related to informational signals. It seems that we have here what can technically be called a "step function," as opposed to a "continuous function" (see Figure 1). This is probably because neglected stocks are more sensitive to new information than the informationally loaded brand-name stocks.

FIGURE 1
Typical Upside Price Move of Neglected Stock—A Step Function

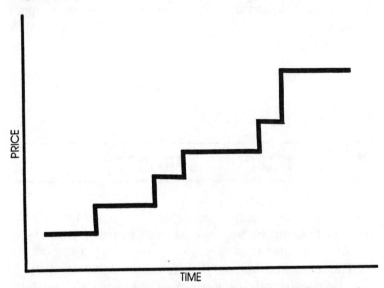

Typical Upside Price Move of Nonneglected Stock—A Continuous Function

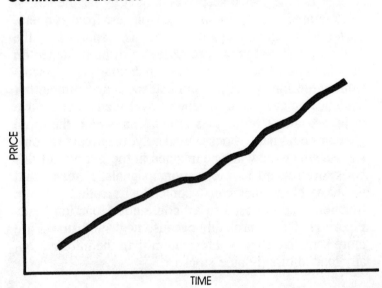

Food for Thought 3:
The Forsaken Front-runners
and Their Home Base

In 1983 the five stocks that had the highest returns for the year as a whole, among all stocks listed in the New York Stock Exchange (excluding preferred stocks), were:

1. A.P.L. Corporation   319 percent
2. Esquire Radio   282 percent
3. International Rectifier   243 percent
4. Hesston   216 percent
5. Gerber Scientific   215 percent

(*Source: The Wall Street Journal,* January 3, 1984.)

You have never heard of these companies? Neither had I, nor had most financial analysts or big institutions. They are all neglected companies.

Why didn't the IBMs, the Exxons, and the Telephones outperform the market? Because everybody invested in them (that is, everybody who really counts, the big guys). By definition, "everybody" cannot outperform the average. They are, in fact, the market.

Let's go one step further: the five stocks that had the highest 1983 returns in the much more neglected Over-the-Counter market were:

1.	DentoMed	2,450 percent
2.	Mtn. Ovrthr.	1,588 percent
3.	Equilink	1,500 percent
4.	Marthnoff	1,100 percent
5.	Lawhon Frn.	1,020 percent

(*Source: The Wall Street Journal,* January 3, 1984.)

Have you heard of these companies?

Has your broker?

Are you surprised that the returns here are much higher than for the NYSE leaders?

Where do you expect returns of the top leaders of the semineglected American Stock Exchange to be? In between, of course.

Indeed, the top fliers of the American Stock Exchange yielded returns much lower than those of the front-runners in the highly neglected OTC market but higher than the NYSE. Exactly as implied by the overall degree of neglect of the various stock exchanges. (The highest 1983 return in the American Stock Exchange was 429 percent for a company named Marshland).

This is the story of the abandoned front-runners and their home base for 1983. Make no mistake about it. In this respect 1983 was a normal year. What we see here is typical.

The Lesson of the Highly Successful Investors

"I can see that there is a lesson or two in all this for making money in the market," you might be thinking now. And what has been presented so far, in terms of the research and testing ideas against observations, supports this.

But perhaps we should add another dimension to it. One way to find success is to study the successful. So what about the following, most relevant question: To what extent have those who have really made it in the stock market, the most successful, indeed followed the neglected stock approach?

This is clearly a worthwhile idea: to study in depth what the very successful have been doing, to try to identify common denominators, and if such exist to check carefully to see if what was feasible for the winners is feasible for you; and then to try to apply it. A very simple idea: follow the successful to success.

Unfortunately, this is easier said than done. First, the really successful do not fully disclose their strategies. They are smarter than that. So, the historical record is incomplete. This means you have to guess a lot. Many pieces will be missing from this particular puzzle.

Second, what was feasible for them usually is not feasible for us. Different people have different resources, in the broadest sense of the term, and face different opportunity sets. Furthermore, investors differ in their temperament and have different skills.

Also, common denominators in strategies are hard to define conceptually and even more difficult to identify, measure, and verify. Some hard-to-detect but critical unique characteristics might draw the line between success and failure. Or, in some cases of success there might be no real common denominators at all.

And finally, the luck component is always at work. How do you control luck—that very distinct, random combination of events that just happens and makes things click?

This is why there are not many such studies. Or, to be more precise, *serious* studies that look for the formula of success based upon analysis of the successful. It is just not that simple.

But let's be a little bit more positive about it. And at the same time answer the question somewhat more directly.

There is one study that I know of that best describes the lesson-of-the-most successful question. This study does suffer from some of the limitations mentioned above. But it still contains a lot of relevant information that should not be ignored. The results of this effort were published in an excellent book entitled *The Money Masters* by John Train. [17] Mr. Train is a successful investment adviser and an author of several books on finance and investments. He also writes a column on financial strategy in *Forbes* magazine.

Mr. Train interviewed nine highly successful investors who had made literally millions, and fame, in the market, and carefully studied their investment strategies and specific policies. In addition to a detailed analysis of the winners' policies, Mr. Train attempts to analyze the common denominators among them. He calls this analysis "The Masters Compared." To me, this is the most exciting part of his effort.

What is his conclusion in summing up the lessons of his masters? He starts with investment don'ts and his first conclusion is *avoid popular stocks.*

"If you buy Polaroid when everybody feels it's cheap," says Train, "you can be fairly sure that the stock is overvalued."

Explaining this point further in more general terms, Train continues, "A glamour stock in a good company (is usually) overpriced because it's everybody's darling at the time. It's hard to make money buying one."

Please note, this is Train's *first* conclusion regarding the lessons that can be learned from the "world's most masterful investors." The message of the greatest money masters—where they put their own money—is loud and clear: avoid the market darlings.

In a somewhat picturesque way, John Train summarizes this point: "A highly favorable purchase is very likely to seem odd, uncomfortable, risky, dull, or obscure at the time when you buy it. Propitious reactions are: 'That dog?' or, 'I can't see it doing anything for the next six months.' Later, everybody gets the idea and feels comfortable or enthusiastic about it. Then it's too late."

What is Train's second conclusion about the masters' consensus of strategies that don't work?

"Avoid fad industries." This is basically the same point but now at the industry level. "Fads and broker's stories are variations on popular stocks," says Train. And, as you might guess, again I couldn't agree more. That's exactly what our many years of research shows.

Mr. Train then struggles with the attempt to identify the common strategies that *did* work for the winners.

Again, the same conclusion applies, now in the positive sense of investment do's rather than don'ts. For instance, the second point in the masters' common do's list is "Buy when stocks have few friends"—and on and on it goes, clearly music to my ears, confirming our own findings from an entirely different point of view: the success record of the successful.

Food for Thought 4: A Premium for Loneliness?

Isn't it possible that part of the higher return of neglected stocks (i.e., the Neglected Firm Effect) is in fact a reward given to investors for having the guts to carefully wander outside the herd? A reward for being innovative, or, if you wish, a premium for loneliness.

Aren't such rewards the essence of the American business system? (Though, of course, harsh, uncompromising penalties for failure are also part of it.) So, why shouldn't we expect to find it in the stock market, too?

So, What Are Generic Stocks?

The idea of the Neglected Firm Effect, its observed magnitude and other characteristics are probably pretty clear now. But what about the concept of generic stocks?

The term *generic* is of course borrowed from the product market. Any dictionary will tell you what it means.

Take for example *Webster's:* "Generic—that is not a trademark."

Or *Random House:* "Generic—not protected by trademark registration."

But there is a lot more to it. In fact, for our purpose these definitions are far from being complete.

In order to better understand the idea of generic stocks, it is important first to fully comprehend the concept as it applies to the product market. The similarities, though not obvious at first thought, are striking. So forget about the stock market for a moment and take a short trip to the supermarket.

The key point is that generic products (or services), as the dictionary definitions suggest, do not have the stamp of approval of a brand name or a trademark. Generics are sold or bought for what they are worth, not for the name they carry. Most of us don't realize that when we buy a product or a service we pay in fact for two components: first, the product itself, say, a can of soup, a watch, a drug, or lodging services when you use hotels, or even education when you go into an M.B.A. program. Second, in many cases you also pay for the name, or the perception that the name represents in terms of the quality of the product or service. Sometimes there is a third component: prestige or snob appeal. For example, Calvin Klein jeans. But let's return to the soup. When you buy Campbell's soup, in addition to the soup itself you pay for the name, the reputation, or in effect, what the name is perceived to represent in terms of a certain level of quality and consistency. The same is true for Holiday Inns: The name guarantees you that there will be no surprises. Note that brand name does not always imply the highest quality. It just refers to a certain identifiable quality.

Or, consider another example: Ivy League universities. One could perhaps have got an excellent education in many non-Ivy League universities for a much lower cost. Students (or their parents) elect to pay the higher price for the name and reputation that are supposed to guarantee certain standards of education and in this case also prestige.

What is the alternative? To buy generic products or services. You can buy a private brand soup, stay in an off-the-road, non–chain-affiliated motel, or send your child to a state university for education—and in all cases pay less. Would you *necessarily* get lower-quality products or services? The immediate answer is no. But the second thought should be "It depends." In fact, you don't know for sure. Sometimes the quality will be higher, sometimes lower, and you can expect some inconsistency. You buy and pay for just the product or service itself. What you see is what you get and usually you don't see much at the point of buying. The rest is up to you to

1. Investigate beforehand—check the experience of others, read and compare specifications, analyze components. And/or
2. Try it yourself—that is, take a chance and see how it works

In both of these cases some costs may be involved—costs in the broad sense of the term, not only the obvious direct monetary cost but also time, aggravation, confusion, and sometimes psychological costs, the bad feeling of being different or "being cheap" and the fear of making a mistake, and all the rest.

This clearly implies that when you buy a nongeneric or a brand-name product, you also buy confidence. On the other hand, when you buy a generic product you are willing to give up some confidence and live with the uncertainty, or you select to reduce the level of uncertainty by checking the product or service yourself.

In general, if you are rational you should follow this rule: When you feel that the cost of checking a product or service yourself, and the cost of living with the residual uncertainty, are lower than the benefit of the reduced price of a generic product, go generic; buy it. And vice versa: If the cost of uncertainty and the effort to reduce it are higher than the benefit of the reduced price of a generic product, forget about it; don't buy. Thus, as in so many other cases in life, you have a trade-off here. It is lower confidence against higher price.

This idea can be presented in simple graphic terms (see Figure 2). Conceptually, you can move along the curve. Slide down, pay less and sleep less; or climb up, pay more and rest in peace. The slope of the curve should represent the rate of substitution between the two alternatives, which might be different for different people.

At this point you might ask, Isn't the additional cost

FIGURE 2
The Generic Product Trade-off

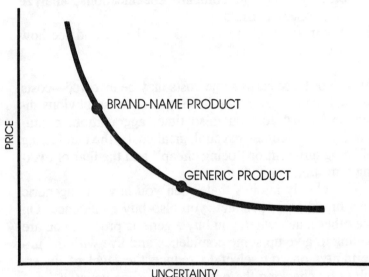

of a brand-name product justified from the point of view of the producer or the seller of the product?

Yes, indeed it is. It takes companies many years and it costs a fortune to develop, maintain, control, and communicate a consistent quality. The advertising cost is only one and perhaps the most obvious cost component. The cost of selecting the appropriate standards and best image, and the cost of monitoring and quality-control, are other examples. Who pays for this grand cost? Obviously, the buyers of the brand-name products.

But on the other hand, isn't the lower cost of a generic product also justified?

Yes, indeed it is, from the standpoint of both parties involved here. The seller can afford to sell for less because he or she spends less on maintaining consistent and identifiable quality. For example, the seller might spend less on quality assurance and advertising. From the point of view of the buyer, the lower cost is also justified and, in effect, required. The buyer has to be compensated for the higher level of uncertainty taken on or the cost of reducing it by making one's own private assessment.

The situation in the stock market is similar, though not identical. We said that when you buy a product you pay for two inseparable components, the product itself and its image or perception. In the stock market, the second component is much more important than in the product market, and in most of the service markets. In fact, when you trade a stock you don't get much of a tangible asset. Think about it. What do you really buy when you invest in a stock?

The product is, in fact, participation rights in several, very fuzzy, conditional, intangible things. You pay for a right to get dividends if and when the company pays dividends. You also pay for a right to capital gains, if and when the stock's market price should be higher in the future than the purchasing price minus commissions (assuming of course that you aren't so greedy you decide to wait for more and end up with a loss). And you also expect liquidity along the way, hoping that a buyer will be found to take your shares whenever you want to sell them, without bidding the price down too much.

You realize that all these rights relate to future events and they are all conditional upon several outcomes associated with the company in question, its competition, the relevant industry, the economy, the market, and the "state of the world" as a whole.

There is a large degree of uncertainty regarding all these factors and not much solid information to go by, but people do have perceptions. Investors have different perceptions, regarding the potential of a company, relative to all other investments that they consider, or regarding the industry and the economy. When they don't agree, a trade occurs. Investors who hold a relatively pessimistic perception regarding a specific stock sell to those who are relatively optimistic. Nobody knows for sure. Given the intangible nature of the traded "product," the level of uncertainty is huge. When you gamble in a casino you can at least find the odds; in the stock market even the odds are unknown to the players. It's all perceptions: yours against others'.

Most of the existing models and theories in the field of investments ignore the perception component, or what we sometimes call *ex ante,** measures of risk. At least they are not incorporated there explicitly. In fact, several models in finance explicitly assume *homogeneous expectations,* or a full consensus among investors regarding the future potential and risk of all companies and their stocks. They also assume that all the usual measures of risk such as price or return volatility, financial ratios, and the beta coefficients are perceived by investors to be identical if they have the same measured magnitude. In reality, however, these measures might be perceived to be different if investors believe that the reliability of the measures is not identical. Put in more technical terms, it is usually assumed that measures of risk for different companies are *equally* reliable and therefore additive. But what if investors consider not only the measures themselves but also their reliability? Or what if not only the content of the information is considered, but also its quality? That's where the brand-name idea (or the lack of it) enters the picture.

Some companies are highly followed by financial an-

*The term *ex ante* is used to distinguish forward-looking, or predicted, variables from *ex post,* backward-looking, or historical, variables.

alysts on a continual basis. Every piece and bit of new relevant information is not only immediately uncovered and assessed but even speculated on in advance. Furthermore, this is most likely the main reason for the informational heaven that exists in connection with these companies, which are widely held by financial institutions: pension funds, banks, insurance companies, mutual funds, investment companies. In many cases these big money people hold more than sixty, or even seventy, percent of the companies' equity. Examples of this group are IBM, American Telephone and Telegraph, Exxon, General Electric, DuPont, and several other blue-blooded brand-name stocks.

Part of the price of these stocks is a hidden fee for the monitoring cost, or for what has been recently called in financial theory "agency cost." Somebody serves as your self-appointed agent. Actually, by definition, the more popular the stock is, the more numerous such agents are. These agents are the hundreds of analysts, investment specialists, and portfolio managers, well educated, and highly specialized, equipped with the best computers, industry contacts, information management systems, unlimited travel budget, and battalions of ambitious assistants who don't leave one stone unturned. The result is informational heaven: blue skies that are practically clear of any clouds that might cover relevant information.

Have you ever thought of who pays for this very professional, efficient, but very expensive service? You do, Mr. Investor, every penny of it! When you buy a brand-name stock, you pay an extra fee for the monitoring services that result in better-quality information, more confidence, and less uncertainty. As a rule, the price of these brand-name stocks, other things being equal, is higher, exactly as in the case of brand-name products and for the exact same reasons, and the return is lower.

What is the alternative? Let's consider the other extreme, and of course, let's not forget that there are many cases in between. One can invest in a generic stock, a stock that is not followed by analysts on a regular basis and does not have the stamp of approval from financial institutions. Not only is the information itself more fuzzy and not continually assessed by the experts but also, since financial institutions have little equity and therefore no control over the company, there is less monitoring of management performance.

All this results in an information deficiency. Please note, it is not that you cannot get numbers for the usual measures of risk like volatility, financial ratios, some earnings forecasts, or even beta coefficients. Of course you can. With some effort you can obtain such numbers for practically every company. But their level of confidence is much lower when the stock is neglected and, what counts most, there is less of a consensus regarding the stock's potential.

The skeptic in you again jumps and bites: How do you know that a lower degree of consensus regarding the stock's potential is in fact associated with generic-neglected stocks?

In the process of researching the Neglected Firm Effect in an effort to understand it better, we found a highly significant inverse correlation between analyst consensus and degree of neglect: the more a stock is neglected by analysts and financial institutions, the higher the lack of consensus (or call it perceived, ex ante risk) regarding the company's earnings growth. This diversity of perceptions represents both a risk and opportunity. This is the area where to be right means a big reward. We shall return to this important point in Part III, where the reasons for the Neglected Firm Effect will be explored.

* * *

Now that we understand *what to* expect we are ready to see *how to* do it.

But before moving to the next chapter let's have a final bird's-eye look at the idea of generic stocks. This is presented in a somewhat oversimplified way in the following chart (see Figure 3).

FIGURE 3
The Generic Idea: Summary

- **In the Stock Market, as in Many Other Places, One Pays for Reputation, i.e., Brand Names.**

- **The Cost of Reputation is Embodied in the Stock's Price and is Reflected in Lower Returns.**

- **Generic Stocks Are Stocks Without Reputation: They Sell for Less and Over the Long Run They Yield Higher Returns.**

- **Since "No Reputation" Does Not Necessarily Mean "Bad Reputation" and "Bad Reputation," Even When it Exists, is Not Always Justified, You Can Sometimes Do Better by Going Generic.**

- **Pre-Fabricated Reputation (i.e., Brand Name) Can be Replaced by Do-It-Yourself Analysis, Diversification, or Both.**

Food for Thought 5: Generic Toothpaste and Generic Stocks

Come to think of it, if generic products exist in the product market and the notion of paying less for non-brand names flourishes all over, from soap to computers, why shouldn't it also exist in the financial assets market?

Aren't factors like stamp of approval, performance monitoring, and reliable information more important for stocks than for toothpaste? If so, the difference in price (return) between generics and nongenerics should be larger in the financial assets market. Consequently the potential benefit of going generic should be higher.

If going generic is good for many people in the product market, shouldn't this also be so in the financial assets market?

Would you say that people who tend to buy generic products would be the most likely investors in generic stocks?

PART II
HOW TO INVEST IN GENERIC STOCKS

An Overview

Before we start with a step-by-step presentation on how to implement the Generic Stock Investment Strategy, let's first see where the previous discussion has left us.

We now know that the Neglected Firm Effect exists; though, at this point, we don't fully understand why it endures. We know that its magnitude is considerable, and that the usual measures of risk cannot account for it. We also know that the outstanding performance of neglected companies persists over time, regardless of whether the market goes up or down. While there is no doubt that the Neglected Firm Effect is related to company size, it prevails over and above size and is clearly observed across all size groups. In addition, there are strong indications that a large proportion of the outstanding performance occurs in jumps and much of that in January. We now understand the idea of generic stocks and how it relates to information deficiency. Finally, we have to remind ourselves that it is very unlikely that anyone will consistently get something for nothing, especially in a competitive environment like the stock market. This implies that there must be a hidden cost somewhere for participating in the generic stock feast.

Any proposal for a new investment strategy to beat the market without a full search and disclosure of its cost, in the broadest sense of the term, is misleading. Recall that, unfortunately, what seems to be free is usually either too plentiful to deserve any price, or useless, or has some hidden costs that in fact make it costly over the longer run. Where does the Generic Stock Investment Strategy stand in respect to this reality? I prefer to postpone the discussion on this irritating point, but not for long. A

FIGURE 4
Generic Stock Investment Strategy
HOW TO DO IT—A SIMPLIFIED LOGICAL FLOW CHART

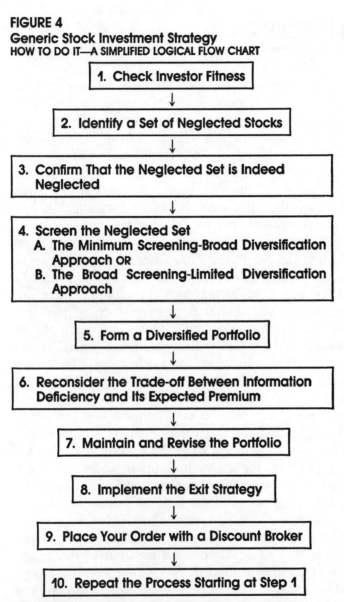

1. Check Investor Fitness
↓
2. Identify a Set of Neglected Stocks
↓
3. Confirm That the Neglected Set is Indeed Neglected
↓
4. Screen the Neglected Set
   A. The Minimum Screening-Broad Diversification Approach OR
   B. The Broad Screening-Limited Diversification Approach
↓
5. Form a Diversified Portfolio
↓
6. Reconsider the Trade-off Between Information Deficiency and Its Expected Premium
↓
7. Maintain and Revise the Portfolio
↓
8. Implement the Exit Strategy
↓
9. Place Your Order with a Discount Broker
↓
10. Repeat the Process Starting at Step 1

REMEMBER: BE CAREFUL! YOU ARE OPERATING ON THE DARK SIDE OF THE MOON!

better understanding of the selection process for generic stocks will help in resolving the cost issue. In fact, as you will soon see, an important component of the generic investment decision is a consideration of the cost side and a careful weighing of it against the expected benefits. So, let's turn to the how-to phase.

The two key questions in this respect are: Should one try to benefit from the Neglected Firm Effect, and if so, how?

In order to be specific and pragmatic about how to implement the generic investment idea, this strategy will be presented as a list of steps that should be followed in sequence.

A summary of the steps and their logical sequence is given in Figure 4. This kind of logical flow chart, like a road map, is designed to give an overview of the area covered, points to be visited, and some sense of direction about which road leads where and in what sequence. The content of the boxes and the logic for the flow will be discussed now.

Step 1: Check Investor Fitness

The first step is to check whether the Generic Stock Investment Strategy does indeed fit you. As with products and services, not everyone is best advised or willing to go generic. Some people prefer to stay in the brand name area.

Before adopting any investment strategy, one has to define the investment goals in the most specific and explicit terms possible. The same applies here. These goals should usually refer to three main factors:

1. Level of *acceptable risk*
2. *Time horizon* of the investment (short-term versus long-term)
3. *Liquidity needs* of the investor

Various combinations of these three factors are possible. For example, for short-term investments you can select high risk (trading in options) or low risk (trading in government notes), and you can choose more or less liquid securities. The same applies for long-term goals. The opportunity set of available securities is so broad that the three aspects of the investment goals, i.e., risk, time, and liquidity, are not binding or mutually exclusive. The choice is completely yours. Just make sure that the combination of objectives that you choose fits your needs and that it is consistent with what you can and want to do. There is no sense in taking high risk, even if the expected return is very high, if you are the type of person who worries a lot. The cost of sleepless nights might be too high. And it is almost guaranteed that fear will lead you to wrong decisions. In this case you'll not only die early but also poor. On the other hand, if you are the entrepreneurial type a more risky investment that requires more of your time but offers higher rewards might be the wise pick.

The Generic Stock Investment Strategy fits many investor goals but not all. As a rule, it fits the more innovative and entrepreneurial investors, individuals who are willing to be original, to explore opportunities yet to be recognized by the traditional investment community. They key point that should be considered at the fitness-check step is the trade-off between a lower level of confidence and a higher expected return. It should be remembered that when you decide to invest in neglected stocks, you choose to operate on the market frontier. Basically, you choose to adopt an entrepreneurial approach. As in the general business field, such an approach is expected to be highly rewarding but it requires certain personal qualifications: ingenuity, perseverance, and the willingness and the guts to leave the herd.

In more specific terms, one should realize that investing in generic stocks typically puts you in a situation in which:

1. Information is less conveniently available on a continuous basis, is less complete, and is usually of lower quality. Therefore, you should be ready to do something about it, that is, screen and diversify. Keep reading; both will be explained soon.
2. There is a lower level of consensus among investors and among analysts regarding the potential of the

neglected companies. Your favorite broker will most probably be quite confused. A frequent response will be "Why do you need this dog?" Be ready to ignore anyone who tries to discourage you.

3. The investment opportunity set, that is, the overall list of stocks to be considered, includes a higher proportion of smaller companies, even though several large and medium-size companies are also neglected at any given time. This could affect the liquidity of a generic stock portfolio. But this is likely only for large block transactions such as those made by the bigger financial institutions. If you are not Prudential it probably won't affect you.

4. The dividend income is lower and often nonexistent—at least for the time being—so forget about dividends. Typically, one does not buy generic stocks for dividend income.

Before you invest, you should refer to these points and decide if you can live with them. For example, a relevant question in this respect is the minimum level of information (quantity and quality) that you require in order to invest. You also have to decide about the effort that you will be willing to put in to eliminate or to reduce any information deficiency, to reach that required minimum.

Remember, delicious as it is, the generic lunch is not free. It is a good idea to face reality before you start and to decide whether you are willing to pay the cost. There is, however, a piece of good news that makes the first step of the fitness test much easier. Not only easier to run but also easier to decide.

In one respect the stock market is clearly unique and different from any other market for products or services. It offers almost unlimited possibilities for diversification. This means that the specific investment decision is not necessarily yes or no but can be in between. Also, by diversification you can offset your mistakes. Somebody smart has defined diversification as follows: "If you can lose everything in one stock and still be smiling at 4:05 P.M. because your total portfolio is up for the day, you are well diversified."

The stock market is, in fact, the only place where one can be half pregnant, or, if you wish, in our particular case you can be "half generic."

When you buy, for example, a TV set—that's it! You cannot buy half of a TV set for just a couple of weeks. Or when you select to go to an Ivy League university, you are usually committed for at least one semester. In the product or service market, the decision to buy is typically an either/or decision, mainly because in most cases there is no continuous divisibility of the product or service unit. Also, you don't have the liquidity that allows you to sell or buy at practically any time. In the financial assets market you have the option of creating unlimited mixes by combining different securities into portfolios, and you can change the mix whenever you want. This implies that the commitment is less binding across time and across products (securities).

For example (and keep in mind the case of the TV set as a contrast), you can decide to go generic by investing *part* of your money in generic stocks, as the more entrepreneurial segment of your portfolio, and part in non-neglected, brand name stocks. Later on if you wish you can change the proportion, based on what you have learned from actual investment results and changing market situations.

The importance of the diversification option cannot be overemphasized. For smart investors the market game is not a "hit-or-miss" situation but rather "hit some and miss some."

The diversification choice should be considered right

at the beginning—when you apply the fitness test—as you might decide that you are just partially fit and therefore choose to try the generic stock idea on a small portion of your portfolio. I call this the Generic Cocktail Option—because in this case the fitness test is not necessarily mutually exclusive in its conclusion, as to whether one should go generic or nongeneric. You can do both!

The Generic Cocktail Option is relevant not only for private investors but perhaps even more for some financial institutions. For various unjustified reasons, institutions have been ignoring this opportunity. Given their size and the typical small float (float is the number of shares outstanding) of generic stocks, financial institutions cannot go generic. There are other important reasons why they cannot do so. But they can choose the Generic Cocktail Option. More will be said about this later, and the amazing story of one fund that has implemented this option will be told (see "Food for Thought 10," p. 150).

Once you have passed the critical fitness test, and decide that you want at least some generic stocks in your portfolio, you can proceed to the next step.

Step 2: Identify a Set of Neglected Stocks

Neglected stocks have been defined in the first part of this book. Now the question is, Where and how can you find them? Four points have to be emphasized here:

1. All available measures of neglect are proxies. They can give you an estimate, an indication, sometimes just a feel for the level of neglect. By no means are they exact measures. It is, therefore, a good idea to supplement the data with some good old judgment.

2. The measures of neglect are relative measures, and should be treated as such. In this context the term *relative* has two dimensions: relative to other stocks, e.g., IBM compared with Yatom Corporation (the maker of the chemical chicken soup mentioned earlier) and relative over time, that is, the change in the level of popularity of a stock, e.g., Apple Computers at the present compared to 1978, Chrysler Corporation in 1980 versus now.

3. Since indeed in many cases the degree of neglect changes over time, the measures should be checked and updated not only before every investment decision but preferably at least every month or so, when the hold or sell options are considered (see "The Exit Strategy," p. 140). In order to maximize the benefits from the Generic Stock Investment Strategy, the portfolio has to be followed, revised, and maintained continually based on updated measures of neglect.

4. Finally, it is better to use several sources and different measures to estimate neglect. I call this "neglect confirmation." More will be said about it later (in "Step 3").

In the following pages some of the better sources of information to identify neglected-generic stocks are discussed. Most of the sources in the list are easy to find, practically free, and easy to use. Some of the sources are not as readily available. However, most good brokers have access to them. So it is up to you to ask—and to insist. Remember also that most of the sources on the list are mutually interchangeable—you don't need all of them. In fact, you have a broad range of choices here; it's up to you to choose.

A LIST OF SELECTED SOURCES TO IDENTIFY NEGLECTED STOCKS

1. Number of Financial Institutions Holding the Stock and Number of Shares Held by Financial Institutions

Source: Standard & Poor's Stock Guide [15].*

Monthly publication. This is probably the easiest and most accessible source of information to determine a stock's relative level of neglect. Many studies, including ours, have shown that by using data from this convenient source the Neglected Firm Effect can be detected. Consequently, it can be used as a base for the Generic Stock Investment Strategy. The data covers more than 5,100 companies and about 2,550 financial institutions including investment companies, banks, insurance companies, college endowments, and "13F" money managers. It provides an indication of the extent to which a company is institutionally neglected. This source is most readily available with all brokers and at many public libraries, or it can be ordered directly from Standard and Poor's Corporation at small cost.

The S&P *Stock Guide* provides many other important data needed for fundamental analysis. These

---

*The numbers in parentheses refer to a detailed reference list at the end of the book.

can be used for screening the generic stocks to be discussed later in "Step 4." In general, the S&P *Stock Guide* is considered to be the security analysts' bible, and is a good starting point for any fundamental analysis.

We found that the data on institutional holding in this convenient source can provide a good tool for identifying generic stocks. Furthermore, there is a high correlation with degree of neglect as measured by the level of attention given to the stock by financial analysts. As a rule, a stock that is held by less than ten financial institutions can be considered neglected. The smaller the institutional holding, the more neglected the stock is. Remember, while the absolute number is an important indicator, the change in institutional holding over time is also important. Thus, for example, a decline in institutional holding from thirty to twenty institutions indicates a reverse in the popularity flow and the stock should be considered for the generic portfolio.

Several other financial information services publish similar data on institutional holding, such as *Moody's Handbook of Common Stocks* [11] and *The Value Line Investment Survey* [18]. These are all equally good, and readily available on a current basis in many public libraries or from stockbrokers at practically no cost. In fact, any other reliable source that provides current numbers on institutional holding can be used.

2. Number of Shares Held by Banks and Funds

Source: Industriscope (Media General Financial Service) [9].

This monthly publication covers data similar to that in *Standard & Poor's Stock Guide* for about eigh-

teen hundred stocks. The main advantage of this
source is that the data is presented by industry
subgroups, which facilitates easy comparisons of
companies within each industry and across industries. Like the S&P *Stock Guide,* this source also
provides many other important fundamental data that
can be used for screening the neglected stocks. It is
particularly helpful for cross-industry diversification—to be discussed later. Some of the data in this
publication (like separate beta coefficients for up and
down markets) cannot be found in any other publication. For those of you who have access to personal computers, the *Industriscope* data is now also
available from the Dow Jones on line, computerized
News Retrieval Data Base.

3. Number of Major Analysts Following the Stock and Reporting Earning Forecasts

Source: Standard & Poor's Earnings Forecaster [14].

The number of major analysts, or investment houses,
following the stock and reporting earnings forecasts
for the company is an important indicator for degree of neglect. Such information is published weekly
in the *Earnings Forecaster.* It contains a list of
leading analysts and their earnings forecasts for over
sixteen hundred corporations. In general, the smaller
the number of listed forecasters, the more neglected
(generic) the stock is. If a stock does not appear on
the list, one can conclude a comparatively low level
of popularity, that is, that the stock is neglected. This
source covers only about fifty *major* analysts. It is
less complete in its analyst coverage than the next
two sources listed below. However, in our research
we have found it to be highly correlated with other
more detailed measures of neglect, and therefore,

while less than perfect, it is a good indicator for neglect in relative terms. This source is also less expensive and more publicly available than the other more detailed data bases on analyst coverage.

4. **Number of Analysts Reporting Earnings Forecasts—A Broader Base**

Source: Institutional Brokers Estimate System (IBES) Monthly Summary Data [7].

This service covers over three thousand companies and thousands of financial analysts. A typical IBES monthly publication reflects more than twenty thousand short-term earnings estimates and about ten thousand for the long term. This is certainly a broad-base measure of attention given to companies. Again, the smaller the number of forecasters following the company, the more neglected is the stock. Given that this data base is much larger in its coverage of financial analysts and companies, it offers a more precise measure of neglect and a better measure of change in popularity than the S&P *Earnings Forecaster* mentioned above. However, this source is much more expensive and less available to the general public. Like most of the other sources listed here, it also contains a treasure trove of additional information, including the dollar amount of earnings forecasts for different future periods of time, changes in an estimates confidence index, and a measure of analyst consensus.

5. **Number of Analysts Reporting Earnings Forecast—Another Broad-Base Measure.**

Source: Zacks Investment Research: The Icarus Service [22].
This source contains information similar to the IBES data. It covers about eighteen hundred companies

and thousands of analysts. Part of this important data base is available now from the Dow Jones on line, computerized News Retrieval Data Base [5]. Zacks Investment Service also supplies customized reports and computer tapes and software. Like the IBES reports, this source provides excellent coverage but it is comparatively expensive and is less available to the general public (in libraries) than the S&P *Earnings Forecaster*. However, most large brokers have access to it through their research department and can provide you with the information.

6. Bank Sponsoring as a Percent of the Floating Supply of Stocks

Source: Daily Graphs [21].

This weekly publication contains information on the percentage of the floating supply of stocks (number of shares available for trading that are not closely held) that is owned by two hundred major banks. This information is given for about three thousand stocks and is updated quarterly. Typically, a low percentage of neglected stocks will be held by banks.

7. Mutual Fund Sponsorship as a Percent of the Floating Supply

Source: Daily Graphs [21].

Provides weekly data on the percentage of the floating supply of stocks that is owned by mutual funds, as reported quarterly and filed with the SEC. This data, as in 6 above, is useful in that it gives a relative measure, in terms of percentage, of floating supply rather than the absolute numbers for institutional holding.

8. Relative Volume Measures as Indication of Neglect

Source: Daily Graphs [21].

This data set provides information relating to substantial weekly jumps in trade volume activity, an important indication of the beginning of a popularity flow. Whenever a jump occurs, the popularity flow has started, at least temporarily, and the stock is no longer neglected. This information can be helpful in making the decision to sell (see discussion on pp. 136–142). A stock is highlighted in this publication if one of the following criteria is met:

a. It was one of the twenty most active stocks in volume on its exchange.
b. The last week's volume was the largest for the stock in the previous fifty-two weeks.
c. The last week's volume was 100 percent or greater than the stock's average daily volume.

Data on volume is readily available in many easy-to-get financial publications including *The Wall Street Journal* and most daily newspapers. The main advantage of this source, however, is that it flags abnormal volume behavior in relative terms.

9. Information on Financial Newspaper Coverage of Companies

Source: Daily Graphs [21].

Weekly coverage of articles on the company or its stock that appeared in leading financial magazines like *Barron's, Fortune, Business Week,* or *Forbes* and the date of that publication. Another source, mentioned before—the Dow Jones News Retrieval Data Base [5]—provides similar information from *The*

Wall Street Journal. In general, the less media coverage a stock gets, the more generic it is.

10. Analysts' Meetings and Press Releases

Source: The Wall Street Transcript [20].

This is a weekly publication that monitors company announcements of stockholders' and analysts' meetings and follows reports issued by brokers, analysts, and professional investors. If a company is in the limelight you can probably learn about it from *The Wall Street Transcript*'s extensive coverage. If nothing has been mentioned about a company for several months (check the Index), the company is probably neglected.

11. A Comprehensive Generic Stock Investment Service

Source: The Generic Stock Investment Service [6].

This new service (for which the author serves as principal adviser) attempts to implement the book's approach, including: identifying neglected stocks, confirmation of neglect, screening for financial strength, growth potential, and diversification advice.

The analysis is based upon large data bases of thousands of stocks and computerized screening procedures. Subscription costs are comparatively affordable.

The unique feature of this source is that it specializes in The Generic Stock Investment Strategy.

Here are a few questions you might be asking now:

—Are all companies covered by the sources on the list?
—What should you do with stocks that do not appear in any of the sources listed? Should they be ignored?

—Should they be eliminated from the neglected set and not considered for investment?

The answer is definitely no. And that's the beauty of the Generic Stock Investment Strategy. Remember, we are looking for the unpopular stocks. It is relatively easy to identify popular stocks. In fact, it is difficult not to bump into them continually. Thus, by extension, stocks that are not included in the various information sources are truly neglected. But you have to confirm it to make sure that the stock is indeed still hidden. This brings us to step 3.

Step 3: Confirm That the Neglected Set Is Indeed Neglected

An important component of the Generic Stock Investment Strategy is a really thorough job of verification of neglect. That is why the third step of confirming neglect is so important. This, along with diversification, in fact, may be more important than anything else. Recall that our research shows that neglected stocks as a group substantially outperformed the market. The only rule that we used in our studies to verify the Neglected Firm Effect was systematically and consistently to select large diversified portfolios of neglected stocks. That was it— no screening, no fundamental analysis, not even any basic selection rule to eliminate the white elephants that might die. The effectiveness of this approach in capturing the Neglected Firm Effect implies that one has to be careful in selecting *truly* neglected stocks. Thus, the verdict for degree of neglect should be airtight. This is the function of step 3.

There are two ways to confirm neglect. In order to be really sure one should follow both.

1. Apply the *overlap* approach. That is, check more than one source (like institutional holding *and* analyst coverage). If the results overlap and several sources are consistent in their message regarding the degree of neglect, you can be pretty certain. If you get conflicting messages, continue to investigate, or even better, exclude the stock from the neglected set. There are enough truly neglected stocks, so why bother with the borderline cases?

2. Another way to confirm neglect is to double-check with additional sources of a somewhat different nature than those previously mentioned. Some of the most important sources to *confirm* neglect are listed below.

SOURCES OF INFORMATION TO CONFIRM NEGLECTED STOCKS

Remember, the following sources are meant to supplement but not to replace the sources listed in "Step 2."

1. Call the company's *shareholder relations office* and ask for a list of recent analysts' reports on the company or any other recent media write-ups. You have a built-in margin of safety here. Usually, the shareholder office is not only fully aware of any meaningful professional or media attention that the company gets but as a rule will be anxious to share it with shareholders or potential investors. That's their job. Furthermore, companies usually want to show that they are in the limelight, that they are popular, or

even better, that they have been discovered or re-discovered. This is exactly what investors in generic stocks want to avoid. As a rule, when the company itself tells you that "nothing has been written recently," you can believe that it is indeed nothing.

2. Call *your broker,* and even better, double-check with another broker. Ask them to review their research files. If nothing much can be found in their recent research files, it is a sign that the company is yet to be discovered. Accept their apology or their excuse (typically presented as a question, e.g., "Why are you interested in this bowwow?") as a buy signal.

3. Avoid *journalists' "darlings"* or consensus stocks—which are often written up in the financial dailies and magazines. Many studies show that one cannot beat the market based on public information. In academic literature this is called market efficiency in the Semi-Strong Form. Which means that once the information is public it's too late and except for market-talks early on with friends at the office, it's useless. The following statement from John Train's book *The Money Masters* [17] is relevant in this respect: "I often save the lists of 'consensus' stocks published in magazines and check the results a year or two later. One may safely expect that they'll do about 30 percent worse than the average."

Isn't it also a good idea to confirm neglect by checking the price/earnings multiple of the stock? you might wonder.

Almost by definition the P/E of neglected stocks should be low, other things being equal. A high P/E by itself might indicate that the company has already been discovered and recognized and its potential is already reflected in the price.

So why not to use the P/E multiple as an indicator for neglect?

This is indeed an interesting point. It is true that many neglected stocks have low P/E ratios and that low P/E stocks, as a group, have indeed been found to outperform the market; this is called the Low P/E Anomaly. However, my recommendation is to use the P/E measure as an important *screening indicator*—to check whether the stock is overpriced—rather than as an indicator for neglect. Some really neglected companies have a very high, or even infinite, P/E. This would be the case if the company is still not making money or is earning just a very small amount—a straightforward outcome of the arithmetics of the P/E ratio. Nevertheless, these companies are neglected in spite of the high P/E. Whether or not to invest in such high P/E companies is another issue. This question is related to the screening process, to be discussed next. Remember, our last two steps were to identify and confirm neglect. Nothing more yet. For this purpose it is better to use the most direct and clearcut measures of neglect. The message of the P/E multiples is too ambiguous.

Food for Thought 6: Admiration and Appreciation

In recent years *Fortune* magazine has been conducting a survey among several hundreds of top executives and other leading experts in business and finance to identify the country's ten best and ten worst companies. The results are published early in January. The ten best are corporations receiving the soundest overall stamp of approval from the leaders of the business community. These companies are the most admired, the big money guys' sweethearts. On the other end, the ten worst are the weakest companies, the rejected ones, the feeblest, the most hopeless. It seems reasonable to conclude that if there is a consensus among the "people who know" that the latter companies are in really bad shape, they should be tossed aside by every smart investor. Why should you even consider the "worst" companies given that the "best" exist? And who can distinguish one from the other better than the experts participating in the survey?

Let's compare the market performance figures for these two groups for the year 1983—following *Fortune*'s publication of the survey results (see Table 7).

TABLE 7   Market Performance of *Fortune*'s Ten Best Versus Ten Worst Corporations, 1983

Fortune's *Best:*		Fortune's *Worst:*	
IBM	+27%	International Harvester	+171%
General Electric	+24%	Pan Am	+124%
Hewlett-Packard	+16%	National Intergroup	+ 97%
Merck	+ 7%	Republic Steel	+ 82%
General Mills	+ 7%	RCA	+ 54%
AT&T	+ 4%	A&P	+ 49%
Eastman Kodak	−12%	Woolworth	+ 36%
Johnson & Johnson	−18%	Crown Zellerbach	+ 25%
SmithKline Beckman	−18%	American Motors	− 6%
Digital Equipment	−28%	Tesoro Petroleum	− 17%
Average +0.9%		Average +62%	
Dow Jones Industrial Average		+20%	
Standard & Poor's 500 Index		+17%	

Source: Barron's, January 23, 1984.

The stocks of the ten "best" companies went up in price by less than 1 percent, compared with a striking 62 percent appreciation for the ten "worst" companies. In fact, four out of the ten "best" companies declined substantially in price while only two of the worst companies went down, and by much less.

How does the performance of the rejected companies compare with the market as a whole? Impressively, their gain was more than three times better than that of the Dow Jones Industrial Average, and almost four times better than that of the Standard and Poor's 500 index. And the most striking conclusion: The selected ten best companies performed far worse than the market as a whole (1 percent versus 20 percent or 17 percent).

Is it possible that their weak performance is related to their being favorites? It is for you to decide whether appreciation is better than admiration.

Step 4: Screen the Neglected Set

Once you have identified and confirmed a set of generic stocks, you are ready to consider the screening process. The term "consider" is appropriate here because you first have to decide how rigorous you want to be with the screening. One might correctly prefer to avoid a full screening and just do some "pruning." Surprisingly, under certain conditions this approach can be just as effective. This is why the Generic Stock Investment Strategy is so appealing: it is easy to implement. First, let's try to understand what the role of the screening process is within the specific context of the Generic Stock Investment Strategy. Then we'll consider the choices.

THE ROLE OF THE SCREENING

The screening serves two main purposes. The first is to exclude stocks that are neglected for good reasons. That is, stocks with a high risk of financial failure or even bankruptcy, which any rational investor should avoid. The objective here is to distinguish between neglect and rejection. Some stocks are not really neglected but are actually rejected by financial institutions and analysts for good reasons. We simply want to identify the lemons.

The second objective is to exclude companies that will not go bankrupt but will not do anything positive, either. The objective here is to identify and exclude the nebbishes, the permanent sleepers that will never move anywhere.

Given the time value of money, once we buy a neglected stock the shorter its discovery period by the rest of the world, the better. The whole idea of the Generic Stock Investment Strategy is to buy neglect and sell a darling. In fact, the best generic stock is a neglected stock of a solid company that will stop being neglected immediately after we have bought it. In the ideal case, we want to just precede the popularity flow. Clearly your objective should be to avoid both the *lemons* and the *nebbishes*.

This can be accomplished by using a combination of two tools: (a) screening and (b) diversification, which can, within limits, be substituted for each other. That is to say, the more you diversify the less you have to screen, and vice versa. But this trade-off is imperfect. Even if you apply most rigorous and extensive screening, it is still a good idea to diversify—at least on a limited scale. Similarly, even if you diversify extensively, it is always beneficial to try to avoid securities of high financial risk by doing at least some minimal basic screening. In the area between these two extremes there is a trade-off between diversification and screening: to a large extent one can replace the other. More specifically, this suggests that there are two different approaches to generic stock selection:

1. *The Minimum Screening-Broad Diversification Approach.* Here the idea is to reduce risk by broad diversification within the opportunity set of neglected stocks that have passed a very minimal screening for high financial risk of bankruptcy. The rest of the risk is expected to be diversified away. (More will be said about this in "Step 5" [p. 122] where the whole issue of diversification is discussed.)
2. *The Broad Screening-Limited Diversification Approach.* Here the idea is to reduce risk by screening each stock as carefully as possible and then to diversify just within the limited set of stocks that pass.

I don't understand, the perfectionist in you might be thinking at this point:

Surely a fully diversified portfolio of thoroughly screened stocks will do better than a portfolio of half-screened, half-diversified stocks?

This is correct, provided you have the resources (and time) to create a sufficiently diverse set of fully screened stocks to use in forming the portfolio. Remember, what might be ideal under theoretical conditions is often unfeasible in real-life situations. So we have to compromise in order to be realistic about it.

Does this mean that the broad screening approach is better than the broad diversification approach? Not necessarily. We should not ignore the fact that even with the maximum money, time, and effort invested in screening, some uncertainty will still remain. This is especially true for generic stocks because they suffer from information deficiency. Furthermore, given the benefit of diversification as a partial substitute for screening in reducing risk, extensive screening might be redundant.

If diversification is so wonderful why can't we just diversify a lot among a large number of neglected stocks without any screening at all? For two reasons. First, most investors do not have the resources to diversify among a sufficient number of securities to completely get rid of the company-related risk. This is specifically true of small investors. It is simply impractical.

Second, and more important, not all the specific risk associated with generic stocks can be diversified away. Remember, we are dealing here with a special segment of stocks that have a lot in common. For one thing, by being neglected, they all suffer from information deficiency and the resulting estimation risk. By diversification within the generic group, this risk can be reduced but not eliminated. The group as a whole is too homogeneous in this respect to benefit fully from the offsetting effect required for complete elimination of risk by diversification. (More will be said about this point when the M/W principle for diversification is explained [see p. 123].) There is no doubt that even if you invested in *all* neglected stocks available in the market—creating a huge, well-diversified portfolio of thousands of stocks—a high level of information deficiency and estimation risk would still exist for this portfolio as a whole. The only way to reduce the bite of this deficiency is to do at least some screening. Remember, the generic premium is not free. You do have to earn it!

So, the best approach for selecting an effective portfolio of generic stocks is a mix between the two extreme alternatives, i.e., minimum screening-broad diversification, and broad screening-limited diversification. The ideal mix depends upon the availability of information, the investor's expertise, the resources available, and personal preference. It should not be forgotten, however, that while the relative emphasis depends on the specific situation in each case, it is important that at least some combination of screening and diversification is applied, keeping in mind the incomplete trade-off that exists between the two.

How can I tell what the right mix is? asks the pragmatist. To answer this question we have to remember that the reduction in risk associated with some diversification on the one hand, and some basic screening on the other, is very large. That is to say, the initial contribution of even very limited diversification or very minimal screening is considerable. Conversely, the risk reduction benefits from both screening and diversification drop off sharply once you pass a certain point. This is like a good wine that improves a lot by aging in the first years and less in the following years. Several studies have shown that a randomly diversified portfolio of about twelve stocks gets rid of well over 90 percent of all the risk that could be diversified away with a much larger portfolio. Similarly, after screening a portfolio of generic stocks for the clear losers, the benefit in relation to cost of additional screening on the margin becomes more and more questionable.

The practical question is, What specific screens should you use for each level of diversification and how far should you go with them. Let's try to answer these questions for the two basic alternative approaches that are presented here. Any combinations are up to you.

BASIC SCREENS FOR THE MINIMUM SCREENING-BROAD DIVERSIFICATION APPROACH

The objective of the screening in this case is to eliminate companies with a high risk of financial failure. There are several established methods for assessing bankruptcy potential. Most of them rely on a historical analysis of various financial ratios.

Two kinds of financial failure prediction models are widely used: multivariate models and univariate models.

The multivariate approach is pretty complicated, but not really necessary for our purposes. It uses several financial ratios that in combination are expected to predict bankruptcy. The best known is probably Altman's Z-score, which is a weighted average of five accounting ratios.* Different values of the Z-score correspond to different historically determined chances of bankruptcy. A company's Z-score below a certain level is supposed to indicate a high probability of failure. How is the Z-score calculated? First, take five financial ratios like the following:

1. Working capital to total assets
2. Retained earnings to total assets
3. Earnings before interest and taxes to total assets
4. Market value of equity to book value of total debt
5. Sales to total assets

Then assign weights to each of the ratios and calculate an index, Z, that is a weighted average of all the ratios found to be the best predictors. By using analytical techniques like discriminant analysis on data of past

---

*See Edward Altman, "Financial Ratios, Discriminant Analysis, and the Prediction of Corporate Bankruptcy," *Journal of Finance,* (September 1968).

success and failure for a large number of companies, one can determine (a) which financial ratios to use, (b) which weights to choose, and (c) which is the appropriate cutoff point for the weighted average index, Z, to determine which companies pass or fail the test of financial solvency.

The multivariate approach is not simple. Luckily, univariate models, which are much simpler to implement, can be used—yielding results that are a good approximation for those of the more complicated approach. The univariate model, as the name implies, uses just one financial ratio instead of many, but it performs almost as well in bankruptcy prediction as the Z-score and other more complicated indicators. This is the ratio of cash flow to total debt. Cash flow is defined as the firm's net profits after taxes plus noncash cost items (primarily depreciation) minus capital expenditure paid in cash but not charged against profit. Total debt includes all borrowing: both short-term and long-term. Several studies show that companies with a cash flow to total debt ratio of less than 15 percent face a high probability of bankruptcy, while those with ratios above 15 percent are basically safe. The higher the ratio, the better in this respect.

The reason cash flow to total debt works so well as a bankruptcy predictor is that it reflects the ability of the company to repay its outstanding liabilities without refinancing. Companies approaching bankruptcy have usually exhausted all their financing options, so that cash flow is their only source of funds for repayment of debts. For example, a company with a ratio of 10 percent could only pay back its liabilities within an average period of ten years (if it survived that long).

Where does the cutoff point of 15 percent come from? you wonder.

It comes from historical analysis of the many firms that

went bankrupt compared to similar firms that did not fail. But, the cutoff number is not cast in stone. Being based on historical data, there is no guarantee that the same cutoff figure will hold in the future. Also, it might be different for companies in different industries. In accuracy tests it has been found that it works better at predicting which firms will survive than which ones will go bankrupt. Thus, when this ratio is used as a screen for neglected firms, the chances of a lemon slipping through are pretty small, based on past evidence. Figure 5 summarizes the steps involved in this simple basic screen.

FIGURE 5
An Example of Univariate Financial Failure Risk Screen: The Ratio of Cash Flow to Total Debt

---

1. Calculate Cash Flow (=Net Profits + Depreciation − Cash Capital Expenditure).

↓

2. Calculate Total Debt (=Total Assets − Shareholders' Net Worth; or sum up all debt items in the balance sheet).

↓

3. Divide 1. by 2.

↓

4. If the results in 3. is smaller than .15 eliminate the stock from the opportunity set. The higher the ratio, the better.

There are many other simple univariate measures that can be used as predictors of financial failure to supplement the cash flow to total debt ratio. Note that by using additional ratios you in fact create your own *multivariate* model.

Other Screens for Financial Failure

1. The *current-ratio* (current assets divided by current liabilities) measures the ability to meet current debts with current assets. The particular ratio found for the company in question should be compared with the average for the industry, or a subindustry group. If the ratio is substantially below the average, this suggests a high short-term risk or liquidity problems. Such a stock should be rejected. *Industriscope* [9] is a handy source of data for this comparison.

2. Several other *liquidity ratios,* such as working capital to total assets; and *coverage ratios,* such as earning before depreciation, interest, and taxes to debt interest can be used to measure the short-run ability to meet interest payment.

3. Also, as a single ratio, *net income to total assets* has been found to be an excellent predictor (the higher the better).

Two more approaches to determine the financial failure risk of companies are to consider the overall *financial strength* and the *safety ranking* of a company—as determined by different financial information services like Standard and Poor's, Moody's, Value Line, and several others. The most convenient services, with excellent records of predicting financial failure, are described below:

4. Value Line's financial strength ratings [18] measure the financial strength of each of the seventeen hundred companies in the Value Line data base relative to all other companies, in a declining scale starting with A+ + for the strongest companies, A+, A, B+ +, B+, etc., all the way to C for the weakest companies. A rating of C+ is considered to be well

below average, and C indicates very serious financial problems. The rating is based on a wide range of financial ratios as well as the judgment of Value Line's analysts regarding several relevant risk factors that cannot be quantified across the board for all stocks.

Among the main factors considered are financial leverage, equity coverage of debt, equity coverage of intangibles, the quick ratio, variability of return, fixed charges coverage, stock price stability, company size, and reliability of the accounting method.

In using this financial strength rating, your objective should be to identify neglected companies, as previously defined, with the highest possible rating. As a rule, a company with a rating below C++ should be excluded as too risky.

5. Another convenient overall measure of risk is the *safety rankings,* also provided by Value Line [18]. It is similar but not identical to the previous measure. Therefore, both may be considered as a double check. The safety ranking ranges from 1 (safest) to 5 (most risky), and 3 represents an average risk. The ranking is based on several factors like stock price stability, the penetration of the company's market, product market volatility, financial leverage, earning quality, and the overall condition of the balance sheet, as assessed by Value Line analysts. Again, one should try to find neglected stocks with a safety ranking as high as possible and avoid stocks with a safety ranking over 3.

The main advantage of the Value Line *financial strengths* and *safety rankings* is their credibility. In addition, they are easy to interpret, straightforward and nonambiguous in their message, as well as easy to get. Value Line's publications are available in most libraries, and practically all brokers have access to them. Recently, these ratings as well as thirty other important variables for security analysis have been available on a current basis on disks for personal computer users. This state-of-the-art computerized system called Value/Screen [19] allows immediate and updated applications of various screening criteria simultaneously, using the large Value Line data base.

6. Still another excellent overall default-risk indicator for a company is its *bond rating,* which can be found for a large number of companies in Standard and Poor's [13] or Moody's [10] bond guides. The bond guides are also easy to get and their message is clear-cut. In fact, a single call to your broker will give you the information.

Unfortunately, bonds of the really highly neglected companies are not rated. This is another example showing that if you want a real generic for a real bargain price, you'll have to do a lot of the investigating yourself. Good, reliable secondary sources are often not available. And don't forget that one of the most important characteristics of the generic stock investment concept is the do-it-yourself aspect. But an important point should not be overlooked. You don't have to take the generic trip all the way to its extreme, and go for the supergeneric stocks or the most neglected companies. Remember, the further you go, the more difficult it is to find reliable information, and the larger the do-it-yourself component. Luckily, however, neglect, like most other things, is a question of degree. In our research we found again and again that the generic frontier starts, in fact, close to home.

Clearly many generic-neglected companies can be

found even among the companies included in the Standard and Poor's 500 index. This is true for every year without exception in the last ten years. Recall that the relatively neglected companies within the S&P 500 universe have markedly outperformed the S&P 500 index as a whole and have shown several times higher returns than the popular stocks in the same universe.

This also applies to the Value Line data base. It covers about 95 percent of the volume of trade of all stocks. While less than complete, it includes at any given time hundreds of relatively neglected stocks.

What about the other 5 percent? you might ask. As in the case of bond rating, aren't the *missing* companies the really neglected ones, which therefore represent even better opportunity?

The answer is yes, no doubt. But, as always, a trade-off exists here, and the question is how far do you want to go, and can you afford to go into the neglected domain. Within limits, the further you go, the higher the return is expected to be. But so are the costs, in the broad sense of the term; the cost of collecting, verifying, and monitoring information (and, in some extreme cases, even the cost of generating the relevant information practically from scratch), not to mention the guts it takes to be an entrepreneur and operate on your own.

But you don't have to go that far. You might decide to take, for example, the Value Line data base and/or the Standard and Poor's as your relevant universe (as far as the generic idea is concerned, this is a compromise but not necessarily a bad one: you're being realistic). This universe *admittedly* does not represent the *most* obscure set—the ultimate generic universe—but, still, it contains enough generic stocks to explore, hundreds at any given time. This is the ideal universe for a person who is beginning to experiment with the generic stock strategy. While the return here over the long run is not expected to be as high as for more neglected companies outside this universe, it is still expected to be higher than for less neglected companies and, most important, it is a feasible strategy to implement for most investors.

So, the message here is clear: Don't go to Spokane (see "Food for Thought 7," p. 116): there is enough to pick not so far from your own backyard.

Finally, as general advice for the Minimum Screening-Broad Diversification Approach, I recommend a conservative attitude throughout. That is, in the process of eliminating the high financial risk companies, it is better to take a cautious approach. When you have a doubt, you would be better off rejecting a company and looking for another more solid generic stock. There are enough of them around.

Remember, risk taking may be good or bad depending upon the expected risk/reward ratio and the investor's preference. But it is *always* bad to take needless risk. The basic screens for financial failure, as discussed above, are so easy to implement and yield a reward that is expected to be so high that it's well worth the effort. So check and recheck and don't compromise.

Recall that broad diversification is a must for the limited screening approach. How much is "broad"? This point is covered below in "Step 5," which deals with diversification. But first let's cover the second screening option.

THE BROAD SCREENING-LIMITED DIVERSIFICATION APPROACH

If for some reason you choose not to apply a broad diversification approach and select instead to invest in just a small number of stocks, you obviously lose some of the benefit of diversification in reducing risk. Consequently, you have to be more careful in the screening process and apply additional screens to those just mentioned.

The objective of the additional screens is to avoid the generic trap.

The Generic Trap

The generic trap is not unique to the stock market. It often exists in the product market, and the smart shopper tries to identify and avoid it. One can find generic products that deliberately or unintentionally are overpriced. Sometimes shrewd sellers dress up products this way and create generic traps for naïve shoppers who think that they are buying a bargain but in fact would be better off buying brand-name or another generic product. The notion that the poor usually pay more is probably partially related to the generic trap.

Recall where we stand now in the generic stock selection process. Presumably the lemons have already been eliminated by applying the screens for bankruptcy and financial risk discussed above. We are left now with a subset of generic stocks that are most probably financially solid. They are not going to die soon. This is fine, and clearly a necessary condition for all that follows. But we are in the market not just to avoid disasters, but to make money. Therefore, the next step is to unveil the two components of the generic trap. These are (a) the overpriced stocks, which are the most probable candidates for decline in price, and (b) the permanent sleepers, or the nebbishes that are correctly priced but, given their underlying business situation, cannot be expected to go anywhere in the foreseeable future. Remember, there is nothing more frustrating for an entrepreneurial investor than to be stuck with a nebbish stock. It puts you in the position of a dinosaur waiting for the weather to get warmer.

Broad diversification can help in this respect. When

you diversify correctly, the traps are at least to a large extent automatically canceled out and diversified away (see detailed discussion coming soon). In this case you don't even have to identify the traps. But what if you are not ready, willing, or able to split your investment among the required number of stocks for effective diversification? Then the only way to reduce the chances of generic trap is by careful screening.

That is, you have first to uncover the traps and then make sure that you bypass them—this is the double role of the broad screening process. It is easier said than done. Unfortunately, many of the generic traps, like most other traps, are very tempting.

Screens for the Broad Screening-Limited Diversification Approach

The screening is done in steps starting with the more critical screens (which also happen to be easier to implement) and moving to broader, less critical tests. The idea is to apply a *stepwise elimination process* by which stocks that do not meet certain criteria are eliminated. The remaining set is screened again for another criterion and the stocks not passing this second screen are eliminated. This process continues in consecutive steps for several criteria until finally you are left with a subset of stocks that have passed all screens. If the number of the selected stocks is too small for even limited diversification, you may either decide not to invest at this time or you can relax your cutoff points for some, or all, screening criteria—implying acceptance of a higher (and perhaps more realistic) level of risk. Conversely, if you end up with too many stocks in the final stage, you might decide to do the opposite and raise your cutoff points by applying more rigorous acceptance criteria to select only the best of the best.

A "what-if" analysis of checking the sensitivity of the end results to marginal changes in the screening criteria (or perhaps just one of them) is always helpful.

The proposed screens for the Broad Screening-Limited Diversification approach are listed and explained below. It is recommended that you implement them stepwise in the order listed here.

Screen 1: Select Neglected (Generic) Stocks

The first step is to eliminate all stocks that are closely followed by analysts and/or extensively held by financial institutions. Follow the procedures and use the sources of information presented above in "Step 2" (p. 76). Your objective is to come up with a large number of truly neglected stocks. Don't forget to confirm the neglected set as explained in "Step 3" (p. 85). When completed, apply screen 2 for the remaining set.

Screen 2: Test for Financial Risk, Default, and Bankruptcy

Eliminate stocks of companies whose financial risk is too high to be included in the generic portfolio. Follow the procedures discussed in the "Minimum Screening-Broad Diversification Approach" section (p. 94), and apply the tests explained there. Remember, this screen is easy to implement and highly cost-effective. So, don't compromise. Now, proceed to screen 3.

Screen 3: The Growth Potential Test

The purpose of this screen is to eliminate stocks of companies with insufficient growth potential. Such stocks are good candidates to stay neglected forever. Conversely, high growth in earnings per share eventually attracts attention and starts the popularity flow, so that's what you are looking for.

The underlying idea of this test is pretty simple: compare the predicted growth in earnings per share for the company with a relevant reference group.

A stock will pass this screening if its expected growth rate is larger by a certain percentage (cutoff parameter) than those of the reference group. For example, using a cutoff parameter of 20 percent larger growth for the company in question than for the reference group, if the earnings per share of company Z is expected to grow in the next three to five years by 15 percent annually, while the growth rate of the reference group is 10 percent, company Z has passed the screen (since 15 percent is more than 20 percent larger than 10 percent).

This cutoff parameter can be changed based on the "survival count" of number of companies that have passed this screen (in combination with the previous and following screens). This is the "what-if" analysis mentioned before. Play with it by moving the parameter up and down (for example, try a required growth rate of 18 percent or 22 percent above the reference point) and see how the number of passing companies is affected.

What can be an appropriate reference group to use as a standard for comparison? This can be any of the following:

1. The relevant industry/subindustry group (e.g., electronics/consumer-electronics, autoparts/autoparts replacement, office equipment/computers and peripherals)
2. A concept group (for example, cyclical companies whose earnings rise and fall with the economic cycle like metals, papers, machinery, autos. Other examples of concept groups include high tech, services, basic goods, recreation, interest sensitive, international, etc.)
3. Some broader universe like average growth for the market portfolio as a whole (all stocks or a repre-

sentative sample like the S&P 500 index stocks). Being so broad, however, this reference group is less recommended.

Sometimes, especially when you face borderline cases, it is a good idea to double-check and use more than one reference group, like subindustry group *and* the relevant concept group. This can give you not only a cross-checking but also a better focus on the specific universe most relevant for the screened company. For example, computers *and* international, if the company in question is strongly involved in computer exports.

How can you arrive at reliable earnings predictions?

You can use your own earnings per share growth estimates for the company based upon data received directly from the company, other direct sources (e.g., government sources for defense contracts, when relevant; suppliers, buyers, people who work for the company, etc.), and your own personal knowledge of the company. Another approach is to use *secondary sources* on growth estimates as prepared, or compiled, by security analysts and financial services. Three excellent sources are described here.

1. Value Line [18] publishes predicted rate of growth in earnings per share for the next three to five years for about seventeen hundred companies on a current, updated basis. Value Line also estimates projected, for three to five years, book value per share, and dividend per share. In addition, as reference information you can check the actual earnings growth rate for the last five years.

2. Institutional Brokers Estimate System (IBES) Monthly Summary Data [7] compiles and publishes growth estimates for more than three thousand companies as prepared by thousands of security analysts. IBES offers not only the average growth rate

based on predictions of practically all analysts across
the country but also the range of their estimates—
high and low, a measure of consensus among analysts, recent changes in estimates—as well as several other relevant pieces of information relating to
growth and how it is perceived by analysts.

3. Zacks Investment Research: The Icarus Service [22].
This source is very similar to IBES. The information can be obtained directly from the company, or
now also through the Dow Jones News Retrieval
Data Base [5] if you have access to a personal
computer.

In addition, your broker can get growth estimates from
other sources through his or her own files or the company research department.

Remember, however, that the further you go to the
neglected ground, the more difficult it will be to find
secondary sources for the growth estimates, the less
consensus there will be, and the more you will have to
do yourself.

This growth potential test (following the previous
screens just described) when completed results in a subset of stocks that are neglected, financially sound, and
have a growth potential larger than the relevant reference group or groups.

But this is not yet the end of the screening. A good,
solid growth potential is not enough for a company to be
included in your generic portfolio. Growth is great. But
how much should you pay for it? That's why we need
screens 4 and 5—designed to check whether the growth
potential is not already impounded in the stocks' price;
testing, in fact, whether the Rolls-Royce is not too expensive.

Screen 4: The Normalized Price/Earnings Test

The purpose of this test is to make sure that the popularity flow has not yet started. We know by applying screen 1 that the stock is still relatively neglected. But what if without attracting wide attention some investors have discovered the stock before you and started to buy and consequently the price has gone up? This might be good for them but not for you. Again, such a stock could be an excellent candidate to become a nebbish from now on, or even worse, since it might be overpriced because of overreaction, its price may go down.

One way to check for this is to compare the current price of the stock with its normal price. Given, however, that stock prices are meaningless without reference to earnings, a better test is the normalized price/earnings (P/E) test.

This test will tell us how the current P/E of the stock compares with its normal historical level. If it is now considerably higher we had better eliminate the stock because this Cinderella might have a prince or two already. A typical generic trap.

The procedure for using the normalized price/earnings screen is as follows:

1. Compute current P/E ratio (by dividing the share price by the most recent annual earnings per share). Or simply take the current P/E ratio from a newspaper.

2. Compute the normal P/E ratio for each of the last three to five years by using the average price (one half of the high price-plus-the-low-price for the year) divided by the annual earnings per share. Then, calculate the average of these numbers for the last three to five years. This is the normalized P/E ratio.

3. Divide the current P/E ratio by the normalized P/E ratio as calculated in step 2.
4. If the result in 3. is much larger than 1, eliminate the stock from the investment opportunity set. This means that either the stock is overpriced or the popularity flow has already started. Conversely, if the current P/E ratio is equal to or lower than the historical norm, you can be sure that the popularity flow has not yet started. Moreover, if reestablishment of the norm is considered likely, then a low P/E ratio is bullish.

Please note that in this test we compare the stock's present P/E ratio with its *own* P/E ratio over time. This is an important screen to capture the dynamic of the price changes. But, important as it is, this test by itself does not ensure that indeed we have avoided completely the generic trap. What if both the normalized *and* the current P/E ratio are relatively high? If this is the case we might be trapped with a stock that was and still is overpriced. This expensive wallflower should also be eliminated. Another, final test is therefore needed to check whether the stock with all its built-in attractions (neglected, financially sound, high growth potential, popularity flow not yet started) is not overpriced relative to *other relevant stocks*. To do so, we take our subset of survivors (which is now probably very thin and tired of tests) and apply screen 5.

Screen 5: The Growth Multiple Test
While the purpose of the previous test was to compare prices of the screened subset stocks across time (compared with their past normal price), the purpose of the growth multiple test is to compare prices across stocks of other companies.

Comparison of price/earnings ratios between companies is often used to identify over- or underpriced stocks. The lower the P/E, the smaller is the chance that the stock is overpriced, and vice versa. The problem with this approach is that it assumes "other things being equal." Of course in real life things are never equal and the level of the P/E is affected by several factors.

As a rule, (a) the higher the company's growth potential, (b) the more dividend it pays, and (c) the smaller the risk, the higher the P/E ratio of its stock should be and usually is. When you compare two stocks and one has a higher P/E than the other, this does not necessarily imply that the stock is overpriced. The higher price per unit of current earnings might well be justified by a larger growth potential, a higher dividend yield, or overall lower level of risk. In addition, there could be other distinct characteristics of the two companies, and their potential, that justify differences in the price that investors are willing to pay for a unit of current earning. This clearly indicates that P/E comparisons can be meaningful for detecting over- or underpriced stocks only if correct adjustments are made for other factors, mainly those mentioned above. We are dealing here with multidimensional comparisons, which are not easy to make.

Keeping this in mind, we propose to apply for the last screen a *growth multiple test* that adjusts for the relative growth potential of the company compared with other companies, but not for dividend yield and risk or other factors that might be relevant here. We have intentionally selected this simplified approach, not only because it is extremely difficult to specify and apply a single measure that is capable of making stock price comparisons simultaneously adjusted for more than one factor, but mainly because a growth-adjusted measure seems to be sufficient for our purposes.

Recall that we have already screened for risk. If indeed we have done a good job, the stocks that have passed this test are of an acceptable risk level. Furthermore, remember also that by deciding to adopt the Generic Stock Investment Strategy, we have accepted right at the outset a low or no dividend income, at least for the foreseeable future. Low payout is clearly one characteristic of generic stocks that the investor has to accept and live with. Consequently, it is an irrelevant factor in the analysis. We of course know that a stock that will never pay dividends, if so recognized by investors, should have a current price of zero. The underlying assumption here is that the lack of current dividend will be compensated by higher capital gains generated by expectations for high dividend in the future.

Clearly, the potential growth in earnings per share is extremely important for generic stocks and it should be taken into consideration when the price of the stock per unit of current earnings (the usual P/E ratio) is compared with that of other companies. Consequently, the growth multiple test is designed to measure whether the price/earnings ratio of the surviving set of generic stocks (which have already passed all the previous four screens) is not too high *per unit of expected growth*. If a stock has a P/E ratio per unit of expected growth, i.e., a growth multiple, that is relatively high, the chances of overpricing are correspondingly high.

The growth multiple for a stock is defined as

$$\text{Growth multiple} = \frac{\text{Current P/E ratio}}{\text{Predicted growth in earnings per share (percent)}}$$

For example, if the current P/E ratio of Yatom Corp. (remember the chemical chicken soup?) is 14 and its average annual predicted growth in EPS for the next three to five years is 10 percent, the growth multiple is 1.4 (= 14/10). Other things being equal, the lower the growth multiple, the better. A stock will pass the growth multiple test if its growth multiple is substantially lower than that of a relevant reference group.

The relevant reference group (or groups) can be selected in the same way as previously explained when the growth potential test was discussed (see p. 106). Namely, you can choose as a benchmark a relevant subindustry group, a concept group, or some broad market portfolio like the S&P 500 stocks.

The information sources for the predicted growth estimates are the same as for the growth potential test (see p. 105).

In summary, the procedure for applying the final growth multiple test is as follows:

1. Take the current P/E ratio from a newspaper (or calculate it yourself by dividing the share's most recent price by the most recent annual earnings per share).
2. Get the best estimate for the expected annual growth rate in earnings per share in percentage points (by using such sources as those listed on pp. 107–8).
3. Calculate the growth multiple by dividing 1. by 2., i.e., the current P/E ratio by the predicted growth. This will give you the P/E multiple per unit of expected growth.
4. Repeat points 1., 2., and 3. for a relevant reference group as explained on p. 106. The growth multiple for a reference group is calculated in the exact same way as it is for individual stock.
5. Compare the growth multiple for the stock (3.) with the growth multiple for the reference group (4.).
6. If the result in 5. indicates that the stock's growth multiple is substantially lower (say by 20 percent) than that for the reference group, include the stock

as a candidate for the generic investment portfolio. If the stock multiple is not substantially lower or, even worse, is higher than the reference group, eliminate the stock from the investment opportunity set.

The threshold of 20 percent below reference is not cast in stone. That's the cutoff that I typically use and it seems to work well. However, you can select another cutoff point or just accept all stocks whose growth multiple is equal to or lower than that of the reference group. In fact, the threshold can be changed relative to your own preference (which might change over time as you gain more experience) and the characteristics of the specific universe of stocks that you screen. In any case, a "what-if" analysis (of changing the cutting criterion and checking the results) is always valuable and highly recommended.

Finally, a note about flexibility and judgment. Remember that the screening process as a whole refers to several variables. You can relax your requirements a bit on one screen if the results of the others for a certain stock are highly positive, and vice versa. For example, if the firm shows much above-average growth potential, and in addition the financial risk is well below average, you can probably accept a higher growth multiple. No doubt, some trade-off between the screening criteria can be allowed. They should be considered in combination.

This completes the screening process for the Broad Screening-Limited Diversification Approach.

If you did a good job you have now a subset of generic stocks that has a high probability of being free of lemons, nebbishes, and overpriced stocks. The chances of falling into the generic trap are small. More specifically, the screened set includes stocks that

—Are confirmed to be really neglected

—Are financially strong and are not expected to default in the foreseeable future

—Have above average growth potential

—Have a current price/earnings ratio not above the stock's normal historical level—indicating that the popularity flow has not yet started; and finally

—Are not overpriced compared with other relevant stocks—taking into consideration the company's current earnings and its expected growth

Remember that all of the above are needed for the Broad Screening-Limited Diversification Approach, while only the first two screens, which are quite simple to perform, are needed for the Minimum Screening-Broad Diversification Approach.

A new financial service, the Generic Stock Investment Service [6], performs the screening as described above for a broad universe of generic stocks.

At this point, you no doubt want to know how much to diversify in each of the two approaches. This leads us to the next step in the Generic Stock Investment Strategy. But first some food for thought.

Food for Thought 7:
Different Approaches
to Security Analysis and
the Screen-to-Profile Approach
(STPA) for Selecting Stocks

In "Step 4," which you have just finished reading, we proposed a screening approach for pruning the universe of generic stocks down to the "best" subset.

It might be interesting at this point to pause for a while and see how this screening approach fits within the broader sphere of different approaches to security analysis. This might help you to decide whether the screening approach suggested here is indeed the best for what you want to accomplish.

There are dozens if not hundreds of specific approaches to security analysis. I recently came across a stock market encyclopedia listing different approaches for selecting stocks with a brief explanation for each. The book is almost as thick as the Bible. Evidently, the one and only "best" approach has not yet been found, or whoever has found it is smart enough to keep it secret.

If you try to classify this mass of approaches, you'll

probably come up with three broad types. They are all based upon completely different market philosophies, though from the standpoint of the pragmatic investor not all of them are mutually exclusive. If you are more interested in the end results of improving performance rather than in the underlying theories, or if you can't really decide which theory is better, you might choose to apply more than one approach, as long as they don't contradict each other.

What are these three main families of approaches?

First, there is *fundamental analysis*. This is the most widely used approach. As the name implies, it is based upon study of fundamental factors that are assumed to determine the company's value and therefore its stock price. The choice of specific fundamental factors to be considered varies among fundamentalists according to their particular approach and many different approaches exist. However, most include such factors as earning and dividend potential, risk measures, the relative strength of the company and the industry, and a wide spectrum of overall economic factors affecting the economy, the market, the industry, and the company.

Based on careful analysis of fundamental factors an attempt is made to determine the "true" value of the company (per share). Then, this value is compared with the current price of the stock. If the estimated value is higher than the price, you buy. The premise here is that by effectively performing this fundamental value analysis (hopefully based on some relevant inside information that you have and others don't), you'll discover a stock that sells below its worth. Sooner or later the rest of the world will recognize the value, there will be excess demand for the stock, and the price will go up to match the true value. Having bought early, you will make money.

In the opposite case, when fundamental analysis reveals that the current price is higher than the "true" value, you should not buy. If you are unlucky enough to have the stock in your portfolio, sell as soon as possible, since under this scenario you can still sell it for more than it's worth. But do it fast before the other guys wake up!

The level of sophistication in applying the fundamental approach differs. Some analysts use complicated formal valuation models, such as econometric models, that require a large data base and cannot be solved without computers. Others use a more intuitive approach with just a few variables usually centering around the price/earnings multiple and relying on a lot of judgment. Regardless of the level of complication, the underlying idea remains the same: a search for underpriced stocks by considering fundamental factors and some causal relationships that are presumed to determine value.

An entirely different approach to security analysis is *technical analysis*. This approach assumes that it is impossible, or at least impractical, to define, measure, and benefit from cause-and-effect relationships in the market. So, forget about fundamental analysis. Instead, watch the symptoms carefully and try to use them as price predictors. There are only two symptoms in the market that reflect the combined impact of all factors. These are: changes in prices and changes in volume of trade. When something relevant happens, price and volume change. This approach assumes that as in medicine the symptoms can give you the prognosis. So try to identify some consistent patterns in price or volume. Since, according to this approach, patterns repeat themselves, you might be able to predict future price behavior. In essence, the technical analysis approach says that the past and present behavior of the market itself is the best indicator of its future behavior. Stock prices and volume numbers maintain a memory with a message. You just have to know how to read it. And, for heaven's (profit's) sake, don't ask the difficult, irrelevant, question: why? Technical analysis is not interested in a cause-and-effect relationship. Find a good pattern and ride it to riches.

Technical analysis is not as widely used as fundamental analysis and it is, for good reasons, pretty controversial.

The third approach, the *random walk,* is so different that it excludes the other approaches. Pragmatic as you might be, you cannot apply it in combination with the two others. The basic premise here is that, at least in the short run, the market pricing process is completely random; every price movement is independent of the previous one and therefore no patterns exist. So, forget about technical analysis. Also, the market is efficient: no underpriced or overpriced securities exist. Price changes occur in an unpredictable, random way and prices quickly and fully adjust to all relevant new information. Therefore, at any given moment, they reflect all available information. So forget about attempting to beat the market using fundamental analysis.

What is left for the investor to do? Just portfolio analysis, and the resulting efficient and optimal diversification. That's all. You don't need to shop around in a world where everything is efficiently and correctly priced!

For the Generic Stock Investment Strategy we have been using the Screen-to-Profile Approach (STPA), which is an offshoot of fundamental analysis but differs from it in its stock selection technique.

Instead of comparing value with price by attempting to do the impossible (specifying some kind of valuation model that, in order to be effective, has to be not only "correct" but also general, stable, and manageable), the STPA bypasses most of the problems involved in that process. The STPA does this by first specifying a profile of the "ideal" stock that is consistent with our own specific investment strategy (i.e., neglected, safe, high growth potential, not overpriced, popularity flow not yet started, etc.). This determines the criteria to be used to screen stocks. We then search the market by applying our explicit and clearly defined criteria. In its ideal version, the screening process should cover a large universe of all available stocks. With computerized data bases and efficient search programs, such a broad screening procedure is feasible. (We now apply it at Cornell University, even in a basic course on investments.) This will result in a selected subset of the best available stocks—"best" according to the criteria specified for the screening process. As was suggested for the screening of generic stocks, the screens themselves and the values of the cutoff points can, and in fact should, be changed based on the results and changing market condition. To do this effectively a feedback learning mechanism should be built into the process.

The main advantage of the STPA is that it avoids the tremendous conceptual and practical problems involved in the detailed specification of valuation models and their empirical estimates.* It can search a large universe of

---

*These problems relate to the underlying assumptions of fundamental analysis, many unrealistic. An incomplete list of these assumptions includes the following: that causal relationships exist between fundamental factors and stock value, these relationships are identifiable and largely stable over time and across securities; that these cause-and-effect relationships can be effectively incorporated into a workable "model" or decision system that is not too complicated but still correct; that the required input variables can be accurately estimated and that they themselves are stable enough over time and across securities to be meaningful; that at least for some securities

stocks and it employs consistent criteria systematically. Furthermore, it is a flexible approach, easy to adjust to different investment objectives or changes in the selection criteria. It is also dynamic—in the sense that feedback can be easily incorporated.

Interestingly, the STPA does not assume market inefficiency. You only look for stocks that satisfy certain criteria. Some of these stocks might be underpriced if a degree of inefficiency exists. Hopefully they will be discovered by the screening process. But this is not a condition here. The selected stocks cannot, however, be overpriced if the screens are correctly defined and effectively applied on a broad-base universe of stocks. According to this approach, a stock can be defined as overpriced if another stock with the exact same profile can be found that sells for less. The screening process is designed to discover the latter and reject the former. If neither exists, that is, if the market is efficient and all stocks are priced "fairly," the screening process will confirm it.

In summary, the STPA is an effective procedure for applying fundamental analysis in a practical way. It is more consistent and systematic than most intuitive fundamental approaches, and it is more realistic in that it does not rely upon valuation models, which are difficult to specify and practically impossible to implement.

The above-listed advantages of the STPA approach apply for all stocks, but even more so for generic stocks. The STPA, if carefully done, will probably take you a long way, but unfortunately, one can never eliminate risk completely by screening—especially when you operate

---

differences between price and value can be found (that is, the market is not completely efficient); and finally that the move in price toward the "true" value is faster and more dominant than the change in the "true" value itself.

in the uncharted territory of neglected stocks. That's why you have to supplement screening with at least some diversification. This brings us to the next step in the Generic Stock Investment Strategy.

Step 5: Form a Diversified Portfolio

As one cannot be too thin or too rich, you cannot also be too careful when investing in the market. Especially when you deal with generic stocks. This does not mean that you should always avoid risk—higher risk is usually compensated by higher return—but you definitely should not take unnecessary risk. Or ignore opportunities to reduce risk, which is the same. A case in point is diversification. You would be irrational, and in fact self-defeating, not to diversify. Within limits it is easy to do (if you don't go for the more complicated diversification approaches, which are usually unnecessary) and highly cost-effective in reducing risk. The screening processes presented above are expected to reduce the probability of failure and increase the chance of success, but they do not eliminate the former or guarantee the latter. Even the surest investments in the world—short-term U.S. government notes, like Treasury bills—fluctuate continuously in price prior to their maturity date. And, given unexpected inflation, you cannot be sure what your *real* return will be even when you hold your bond until maturity. The further you go from this lowest-risk invest-ment into higher-risk securities, the more critical it becomes to diversify—especially when you cross the border into the generic area where the screening is more difficult to do and its outcome is less reliable because of information deficiency.

Luckily, even in this dubious market segment there are three key things that you do know for sure, and all lead to one clear conclusion: diversification. First, you know that in the future some stocks will go down in price and some will go up; there is no doubt about it. By diversi-fying you are more likely to hold some of each. Second, studies have shown again and again that on the average neglected stocks, or stocks chosen according to surro-gates for neglect such as small companies, low-priced stocks, and low P/E stocks substantially outperformed the rest. So on the average a portfolio of neglected stocks is expected to perform well. Third, the "M/W" princi-ple is true by definition.

This last reference, to the M/W principle, is actually a highly simplified way of presenting the underlying idea of modern portfolio theory—the Markowitz Mean-Vari-ance Portfolio Model. Let's consider two hypothetical stocks that in combination represent an ideal case for diversification: one whose prices and returns behave over time like an *M;* that is, price first goes up a lot, then there is some correcting and it goes down a bit, and then up again and down all the way, like the shape of the let-ter *M* (see Figure 6).

Now imagine a hypothetical case of another stock of a company whose price behaves over time like a *W,* that is, in exactly the opposite pattern. When stock M goes up, W goes down at the same magnitude and with the same timing. In fact, W is an inverse image of M.

Remember that risk is defined in terms of price or re-

FIGURE 6
The M/W Case for Diversification—An Ideal Situation

An M Stock: High Risk

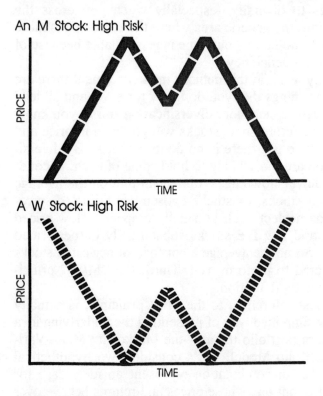

A W Stock: High Risk

An M+W Portfolio: No Risk

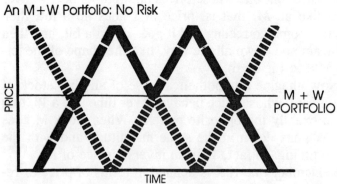

turn volatility. Therefore, stock M is as risky as stock W, though they have different timing in their volatility.

Now, what will happen if you combine stocks M and W in a portfolio of fifty percent stock M and fifty percent stock W? Look at the last graph in Figure 6. It shows the obvious: the line bisecting the *M* and the *W* represents the return of the portfolio that combines the two securities in equal weights. This line is straight and flat as can be.

The conclusion is clear. In this hypothetical ideal case one stock's volatility (risk) is completely offset by the other stock's volatility and risk is totally diversified away. The portfolio of the two stocks has zero risk as represented by the straight line with no fluctuations at all. And please note, this result was accomplished just by diversification—no fundamental analysis, no screening.

This is clearly a fantasy. Of course, in reality it is very difficult, if not practically impossible, to find stocks in an exact "M/W"-type relationship to each other. But the model is a good one to reflect upon, to help understand the benefits of diversification under perfect conditions. The less extreme, and less ideal, cases occurring in real life behave according to the same principle: in a sufficiently diversified portfolio the return variations of individual stocks tend to cancel each other out. Not completely as in the ideal case, but to a large extent. Consequently, the resulting benefit, in terms of risk reduction, is also less striking; risk is not completely eliminated, but still it is greatly reduced.

But how much diversification is needed? According to one approach to portfolio management that was popular in the seventies, and is still widely used today, one is better off doing away with screening and fundamental analysis completely and diversifying extensively. That is, investing in a portfolio of all available stocks, or the "market portfolio." This unmanaged approach to portfolio management, an offshoot of the Capital Asset Pricing Model, is called *indexation:* full diversification and no screening of individual securities at all. It has some merit; by definition the market portfolio, which contains representatives of all stocks listed in the market in the same proportion that they are available, will have only the market-related risk (the "beta risk"). Such a portfolio will not have any company-related, or unsystematic, risk. That's what makes it so attractive to many portfolio managers. You are sure to make the market return. The nonmarket risks—all evils, misfortunes, and even disasters that are company-related—are completely eliminated. The rotten apples will be offset by the really sweet and juicy ones—and in the long run you'll perform just fine.

It seems that the idea of the market portfolio calls for a huge portfolio of thousands and thousands of stocks. Conceptually this is so, but in practice it is not. Why? Because one can easily approximate the market portfolio by using basic sampling techniques, or even by a simple random selection of stocks.

Recall that several studies have shown that on the average as few as about twelve stocks, randomly selected from the market universe as a whole, are enough to eliminate most of the company-related risk. Thus, they approximate the market portfolio.

We have to remember, however, that our starting universe of neglected stocks is not representative of the market as a whole but rather, being a very special subset, all of our stocks will have a lot in common. Consequently, diversification within this subset is expected to be less effective than if it were across all stocks. There is some specific risk common to all generic stocks, which cannot be completely eliminated by diversification within

the generic subset itself. This leads to two practical conclusions regarding adequate diversification.

First, as you already know, you will be better off by
not relying on diversification alone. Some basic screening is recommended even with broad diversification. And
second, diversification should always be broader for generic stocks than for portfolios representing all kinds of
stocks. This is true for every level of screening.

It would be misleading to recommend an exact number of stocks for diversification that will be always correct. Much depends on the magnitude of the offsetting
effect expected for each mix of stocks (technically called
the covariance matrix). This also depends on how effective the screening process is in reducing risk. Taking all
these factors into consideration, I recommend at least
fifteen to twenty generic stocks for the Minimum
Screening-Broad Diversification Approach and at least
eight to twelve stocks for the Broad Screening-Limited
Diversification Approach.

You can improve the effectiveness of the diversification by making an effort to select stocks that are as close
as possible to the M/W ideal. A true cross-industry or
cross-concept diversification can help. For example, many
industries are interest-rate sensitive, among them construction, the automobile industry, other manufacturing
industries, banking. Consequently, diversification across
these industries in a period of high fluctuations in interest rate will accomplish nothing. This is like investing in
the same company under different names. So, make sure
to check the economic substance, the underlying conceptual business situation, and don't go just by names
or industry codes. Remember, simplistic as it is, what
you are really looking for are the nonmatching, M/W odd
couples, or their close relatives. The less they fit each
other, the better they are for diversification and the fewer

are needed in your portfolio. The more effective you are in finding offsetting securities (and the more certain you are about it), the smaller the portfolio can be. Recall that in the ideal hypothetical case of M/W stocks presented in Figure 6, just two stocks were needed to get rid of *all* the risk. But that's for textbooks. In real life you need more.

Thus, the suggested ranges of fifteen–twenty stocks and eight–twelve for the two screening/diversification approaches are not cast in stone. You can move the numbers up or down and apply more or less diversification based on the magnitude of the offsetting impact for every combination of stocks, the effectiveness of the screening, and your own cumulative experience and attitude toward risk taking. Once again, you cannot avoid the need to exercise good judgment.

Finally, you should not forget that diversification, important as it is, is not without its own cost. As always, there is a trade-off. There is a cost for overdiversification (like higher transaction costs, follow-up costs, cost of confusion). So diversify, but keep your portfolio to a manageable size.

Step 6: Reconsider the Trade-off Between Information Deficiency and Its Expected Premium

Now that you have completed the screening and the diversification, you have a better idea of the known and unknown in your opportunity set and you have an idea of how it all fits together in terms of the mix: the portfolio.

This is the time to reconsider the initial trade-off. At this point you might decide (a) to quit dry, that is, not to apply the Generic Stock Investment Strategy, (b) to go generic all the way and to invest in the generic portfolio as identified and screened in the previous steps, or (c) to go for the Generic Cocktail Option by investing part of your money in a reduced-size generic portfolio and the rest in brand name nonneglected stocks and other securities like bonds, mutual funds, or money market funds.

What should a beginner do, a person who has never intentionally applied the generic approach? Here, as in many other delicate situations in which the correct combination of personal preference and individual ability is critical, it is best to learn by experience. Try it first on a small scale and see if it is for you. It requires work, continual attention, perseverance, and an innovative attitude. Help your luck and your portfolio might grow big. But don't put all your money on a one-way ticket before you check where it will take you. Therefore, the Generic Cocktail Option is highly recommended.

Note that in our sequence of steps for implementing the Generic Stock Strategy you are now at the moment of truth: the time when you call your broker and place an order.

This is the time to remind yourself of the golden market rule—so basic that it sounds like a cliché, but, unfortunately, so often ignored:

IN THE MARKET NEVER INCREASE YOUR EXPOSURE
BEYOND
WHAT YOU SHOULD AND CAN FEEL COMFORTABLE
WITH.

If you won't follow this rule you are bound to end up poor or unhappy and most probably both.

The screening and the diversification are supposed to take care of the first part of the rule. Now you have to decide about the second: do you feel comfortable with it?

Many years of experience tell me that overlooking this simple, almost obvious rule is the main reason for market failure. Many times investors are too greedy or cannot take the unavoidable anxiety. If the trip to heaven will kill you, don't take it.

Food for Thought 8: How Far to Go? Are the Cloud Mines of Spokane Too Far?

For years I have been interested in the Spokane Stock Exchange as an ultimate case of obscurity.

Don't be surprised if you have never heard of the Spokane exchange. It is not frequently mentioned in *The Wall Street Journal*. Nevertheless, it does indeed exist in Washington State.

The Spokane Stock Exchange is probably the most neglected stock exchange in the United States if not in the world; it is a place where the most obscure stocks are traded. That's why it is interesting as an extreme case in point. Some really fuzzy, neglected stocks are traded there. The wallflowers of the penny stocks. The neglected stocks that we have researched and I have discussed so far in this book look as if they had won the Oscar (or the Dow) for market popularity compared with what you can find in Spokane, Washington.

Some people claim that there are very exciting investment opportunities in Spokane, but a lot depends on how you define excitement. I was told that over half of the Spokane-traded issues tripled in price at least once from their 1982 lows. Better not to ask about the other half.

In Spokane you have to be unconditionally optimistic.

Let me briefly tell you the story of the Spokane Stock Exchange. It is located on the second floor of an old building on Post Street. The exchange occupies two rooms and a walk-in closet in which all the records are kept. There are about thirty-five listed issues and over one hundred unlisted stocks. The volume is unclear because nobody really keeps records. Until recently there was not even one computer or terminal there. The trades are manually posted on a long green chalkboard facing the exchange gallery in which a handful of elderly men, mostly retired silver miners, are usually watching the action.

Typically, regional, nonproducing-mine stocks are traded, just as they were eighty-seven years ago when the exchange was established. Except that then some of the mining outfits were still alive and operating. Not anymore. The companies traded in Spokane are so tiny, so airy, so invisible that the most and usually the only tangible proof of their existence is their stock certificates. Practically no information is available on the companies, except whatever exists in the walk-in closet. And you won't find much there.

This whole marketplace is so obscure that even the Securities and Exchange Commission has a minimal impact on its operations, and it seems that the SEC gave up trying long ago. Typically, all trading is done on gossip and tips. This is not a case of information deficiency. This is informational chaos. The level of consensus there is comparable to that between Mr. Begin and Mr. Arafat.

Even in Spokane things are relative. The Spokane Stock Exchange has its own over-the-counter market. The OTC stocks are traded there but not listed. These, in fact, provide most of the action. If in New York expectations and perceptions are traded, here fantasies are the going goods. Not sand castles but air palaces—the products of dreaming minds. The unlisted issues are not even supposed to be registered with the SEC and, therefore, they don't have to comply with any minimum reporting requirements—except to the exchange closet. The Spokane OTC has more rumors than the number of stocks traded there multiplied by the number of traders.

The exchange and its listed and unlisted silver mining stocks briefly deserve your attention because they represent the ultimate extreme, and a caricaturelike enlargement of the negative aspects of the generic stock phenomenon: information deficiency, short on record and long on promises, and lack of effective controls. "There is no quality in that market," somebody said about the Spokane market, "but when the wind blows even a turkey flies."

The story of this exchange is a way of better understanding the limits of the generic idea, of pointing out the red line that one shouldn't cross: the borderline between opportunities and bubbles. As in anything else, one should not go too far. Supergeneric stocks should be avoided. Covered as they might be, there are enough gold mines around, so why go for cloud mines? For kicks maybe, but not for investment.

Step 7: Portfolio Maintenance and Revision

THE GENERAL IDEA

You have passed the moment of truth and invested in generic stocks. Obviously, this is not the end of the story. You have now to maintain your portfolio.

What's the difference between a clever person and a smart one? When the clever person faces a problem he or she knows how to get out of it. The smart one knows how to avoid problems in the first place. Since it is impossible to always be smart, try at least to be clever. That's the idea of portfolio maintenance.

At the heart of any portfolio maintenance is the question of timing: when to sell, stay liquid, or switch to new opportunities. This is especially important for generic stock portfolios where more action is expected. Also, the sleepers might die on you. You don't want to keep them longer than necessary.

How should the portfolio be followed and revised?

How long should you hold each specific generic stock that you have in your portfolio?

When should you take profits and look for new winners?

And when should you get rid of the losers and save your neck?

A typical mistake made repeatedly by investors is that they don't pay enough attention to their portfolio maintenance. Many investors spend a lot of effort in selecting securities. Some also carefully consider the attributes of the mix in terms of the diversification characteristics of the portfolio. But then the portfolio is often left alone as if the market were not in continuous flux.

In my consulting experience I have seen so many petrified portfolios that sometimes I feel like an archaeologist. These portfolios may have been excellent several years ago, but they do not represent an attractive investment anymore.

We can define portfolio management, or maintenance, as a continual process of portfolio selection. The stocks you own should be considered as part of the investment opportunity set. They differ from all other stocks only because their opportunity costs are somewhat lower: you have already paid the commissions and the search cost to collect the information. But otherwise they are like any other stocks. If you are convinced that they have a better potential than alternative investments, keep them. If not, sell them. Transaction costs, i.e., commissions and taxes, should, of course, be taken into consideration. But that's it: no emotions. Never marry a stock.

In a somewhat simplified but practical way, one can sum up the whole maintenance phase with one simple question:

"HOW LONG SHOULD I HOLD THEM?"

How do you know when the stock is at its high and whether it won't go higher within the foreseeable future? Or, conversely, at its low and won't go lower?

Let's try to answer these questions by first (again) considering an ideal, happy case:

We have invested in a small, zesty generic portfolio

of screened, relatively safe stocks. They all have outstanding growth potential, and the market is fully coop-
erative; it cannot avoid growing earnings for long.
Consequently, the earnings growth and the other distinguished qualities of at least some of our stocks slowly
attract the attention of analysts and institutional investors. This starts the popularity flow that from now on
bursts up with a mighty push fed by its own momentum.

You, the smart owner of this winning portfolio, should
now be on the alert. You have much more to do than
just sit on your glory and share market war stories with
friends in the office. The battle is not over yet. Remember, you want to hold the stocks only as long as the
popularity flow continues. Frequently stocks like butter-
flies get tired fast. Or, even worse, they die. You have
to monitor continually the number of analysts and institutions following the stocks, among other measures of
popularity, to identify any weakening in the price momentum.

Or, conversely, consider the opposite scenario: the
popularity flow does not start for a long time and snor-
ing is about the only thing you hear from your stocks.
Again, you have to develolp a set of indicators that will
signal when you are stuck with sleeping nebbishes.

We have just stated the general principle. Now let's
look at details. An overview of these is listed in
Figure 7.

MONITOR THE POPULARITY FLOW—
WHEN NOT TO SELL

When you manage a portfolio of generic stocks, you
continually have to diagnose each stock's position relative to the popularity flow. Your objective is to ride the

FIGURE 7
Maintenance of Generic Stock Portfolio:
An Overview of Steps to Follow

---

1. *Monitor the popularity flow:* identify the position of each stock vis-à-vis its popularity flow.

    Using a. neglect measures (see Step 2, p. 76, and Step 3, p. 85) and/or

    b. the price momentum test (p. 138).

2. *Ride the popularity flow* as long as it continues. Divest when the popularity flow dies out (see Exit Strategy, p. 140).

3. *If popularity flow never starts,* divest, following the exit strategy.

---

flow as long as it lasts. That is, you try to buy a neglected stock about to be discovered, benefit from the dynamic move from neglect to popularity, sell, and then repeat with another neglected-yet-to-be-discovered stock.

There are basically two ways to monitor the position of a specific generic stock in relation to the popularity flow. One is to monitor the primary measures of neglect discussed in "Step 2" and "Step 3," namely, the changes in analyst attention or institutional holding. The other is to monitor changes in prices. When price goes up markedly, over and above the market as a whole, one can safely conclude that the stock has been discovered and has become more popular.

These two sets of signals tend to move together, though not at the same pace; one typically leads to the other and they convey somewhat different information. The use of the price indicator has some advantages because this measure is more immediate and sensitive in its response. It continuously reflects shifts in investors' opinion, and that's what we need here. Also, information about price changes is, of course, more current and readily available. But there is merit to the other measures, too. They have predictive power. Usually analyst attention and institutional holding increase *before* changes in prices, so these too can serve as indicators. However, the effective use of these indicators, like any others, depends on availability of immediate and current data on analysts and institutions for follow-up. Unfortunately, such data are not available on a daily or even weekly basis.

That's why prices should be carefully followed as the main indicator for monitoring the popularity flow. The direct measures of popularity/neglect can be used as a supplement, to identify the potential of the popularity flow to continue. This deserves some explanation.

First, how can stock prices be used to monitor the popularity flow?

A measure of *price momentum* can easily be computed, or just taken from financial services publications (see below). You can calculate the price momentum yourself by applying the steps listed in Figure 8. Price momentum with a ratio greater than 1.0 indicates a recent upward trend in the stock's price. But to be meaningful, the price momentum should have a ratio over and above that of the market as a whole. That's why we compare it with the price momentum for some market index. If a previously neglected stock shows a marked upward trend over and above the market trend, then it is in the process of riding the popularity flow and it should be held as long as its momentum continues.

Luckily there are convenient sources for finding the

FIGURE 8
Monitoring the Popularity Flow: The Price Momentum Indicator

---

1. Calculate the most recent four-week average price.

2. Divide 1. by the recent fifty-two-week average price to obtain the price momentum.

3. Follow the same calculation in 1. and 2. for some market index (like the Dow Jones Industrial Average, the S&P 500, etc.).

4. The stock is riding the popularity flow as long as the result in 2. is

    a. Substantially larger than 1.0 (and as a rule, the higher the better), *and*

    b. Substantially larger than the results in 3., for the market as a whole. Again, the higher the better.

---

price momentum. In fact, you don't have to do the calculations yourself.

Several investment services provide measures of the recent price trend. The most prominent (and handy) is Value Line. Their equivalent measure for price momentum is called *relative price strength*. It is very similar to the one proposed here. The Value Line relative price strength can be found for about seventeen hundred stocks in *The Value Line Investment Survey* [18]. This is the same weekly investment advisory service previously mentioned. The relative price strength is based upon

month-end comparisons of stock prices with a broad
market index, the Value Line Composite Average. The
computations are all done by Value Line; they divide the
current month-end price of the stock by the price of the
preceding month. The same calculation is done for the
Value Line Market Index. (Value Line uses its own
Composite Index for this purpose.) The result for the
company is then divided by the result for the market.
The monthly numbers so computed are then com-
pounded from a starting index of 100. Prices are of course
adjusted for split when relevant.

This measure shows exactly what its name implies:
relative strength of the stock price compared with the
market. It is presented in convenient graphs. One glance
is sufficient to detect price momentum: whenever the
graph goes sharply and consistently up, you have price
momentum. Very simple and easy to interpret. As long
as the popularity flow continues, tell your friends how
successful you are and enjoy the ride. As the farmers
say, Make hay while the sun shines.

Now you know when not to sell. The trick, of course,
is to know when to sell. You cannot buy a yacht or even
a bagel with paper profits. This leads us to the next step.

THE EXIT STRATEGY—WHEN TO SELL

As many experienced investors will tell you, and I am
sure you have many times felt so yourself, the sell decision is often harder than the buy. And it is no less critical. When asked why he was so wealthy, Baron
Rothschild said, "I always sold too soon."

There are two reasons for selling a stock other than
for liquidity needs: either things went well and it's time
to take profits, or things went wrong and it's time to save
your neck. It's relatively easy to divest when things have

gone well, more or less according to plan. In the case of generic stocks, if the price momentum continues until the stock becomes highly researched, taking a capital gain on the rise in price just when the popularity flow dies is a pleasant exercise.

But if the price momentum reverses itself after investment, if the popularity flow never materializes and the stock languishes in neglect, then what? That is when the discipline of a well-defined exit strategy becomes critical. One such strategy is outlined on Figure 9.

FIGURE 9
Generic Stock—Exit Strategy

After Riding the Popularity Flow,

Sell When *Both* of the Following Conditions Are Satisfied:

1. Price Momentum is Declining Below Unity and Below the Price Momentum for the Market (see Figure 8, p. 139).

2. The Stock is Intensively Followed by Analysts and/or Widely Held By Institutions (i.e., Stops Being Neglected).

When the Popularity Flow Never Materializes,

Sell When *Either* of the Following Conditions Are Satisfied:

1. Earnings Start Declining.

2. Price Momentum is Substantially Below Unity and Below the Price Momentum for the Market (see Figure 8, p. 139) for Three Consecutive Months.

Why do I propose, in Figure 9, to sell only when *both* conditions 1. and 2. are satisfied for a stock that has started the popularity flow? Clearly, when the stock benefits from a wave of popularity, the investor should try to get the most out of it. If the price momentum declines before the stock is highly researched, it's better to remain invested in anticipation of a turnaround in the price trend, provided the earnings growth remains strong. Also, if the stock is heavily followed, but the price momentum continues, there's no point in selling until the price trend flattens out. The investor should exit, however, once the stock is both widely followed and the price momentum is declining. This stock has probably turned into a brand name. It is no longer generic and is apparently overpriced—at least for you, the entrepreneurial investor. Mission accomplished, get out! And look for another opportunity.

The more difficult exit decision occurs when, after an initial increase in price momentum, the popularity flow does not materialize. The sell decision, or lack of it, in this situation, will separate the successful investors from the unsuccessful. The successful investor will follow a well-defined exit strategy, dispassionately, without allowing emotion or intellectual pride to prevent timely divestment. Here is when you really need guts. In the absence of a popularity flow, if either the earnings growth or the price momentum consistently reverses itself, the stock must be sold.

Food for Thought 9: A Warning About Technical Staff, Opportunity, and Judgment

This is a warning note for you to consider before we move to the last step in the generic stock investment decision process.

The discussions on the screening process, diversification, and exit strategy you have just read were somewhat technical. In general, technical presentations can be misleading. Especially when related to the market. It looks so precise, even scientific, with steps to follow in sequence, formulas, cutoff points, supporting evidence from empirical studies, exit signals, and all the rest. But make no mistake about it. These procedures, like many others used by investment analysts, are just decision *support* tools. They are designed to help you make better decisions, to improve your judgments. Fortunately, however, they cannot replace judgment.

I say fortunately, because making your own judgment calls is where the challenge and the rewards are. In fact, that's what the Generic Stock Investment Strategy is all about! It is a do-it-yourself approach. Your own selections based upon your judgment rather than the prepackaged, consensus-wrapped brand-name prima donnas.

Let's not kid ourselves. The better you are at it, the higher the reward. All the tools, the models, the screens with their magic cutoff threshold numbers and all the fancy equations and signals can help. But only as support for intelligent and creative judgment. The decision making process cannot be completely mechanical. Otherwise every bookkeeper would be a millionaire.

There is no black box (or even computer) into which you plug some numbers, then shake and get guaranteed vouchers for making money. So, use the procedures offered here as support for your judgment. Be flexible and open-minded. Let it age and improve over time by continually incorporating feedback from your own learning process. Be an entrepreneurial investor.

Step 8: Place Your Order with a Discount Broker

This is another key component of the Generic Stock Investment Strategy. The brokerage industry has proved that anybody can be an investment adviser. Discount brokers have proved that nobody really has to be. As a rule, generic stocks should be bought from a discount broker.

A discount broker is equal to a full-service broker in every way except that he or she is not equipped to offer you the research services and specific buy and sell recommendations. You are doing the research yourself, selecting what to buy and when. You also manage your own portfolio and make the sale decision. A typical discount broker will never call you. You are expected to call the broker to place a transaction that you yourself have initiated. (Haven't you noticed that full-service brokers keep calling you? Doesn't it indicate that they need you more than you need them?)

When you have a discount broker, in contrast to a conventional broker, securities are indeed bought and not sold, but otherwise you get all the services. Usually, your telephone calls are answered promptly by people who are fast in getting your order to the trading floor. You typically get a complete monthly report on the status of your account, and most discount brokers now have the computer facilities to update accounts immediately to reflect all changes that you need to know to make current trading decisions. Also, many discount brokers offer immediate loans on your stocks, or margin accounts, at rates that are competitive with conventional brokers. In many cases, securities held in customer accounts are insured up to a prespecified amount.

The key point is that if your stock is truly generic you will not get much information from a full-service broker anyhow. So why pay the additional commission? Using the services of a full-service broker contradicts the underlying idea of the Generic Stock Investment Strategy. And the savings are substantial. For example, for a typical transaction of 1,000 shares at $10 per share with a conventional full-service broker the commission is $249. For the same transaction some discount brokers will charge only $60 to $70—a saving of about seventy percent. A much larger saving of up to ninety percent is offered for large transactions. (While the rate structure varies considerably in this competitive industry, this will give you an idea of the saving.)

How do you find a discount broker? It's easy. Several ads appear every day in the financial press. Before selecting a discount broker, however, be sure to check the company's financial solvency, reputation, and insurance coverage for customers' accounts. Other things being equal, it is a good idea to go with a large discount broker rather than a small one.

This is the last step in applying the Generic Stock Investment Strategy. It is consistent with all the rest. Don't pay for things you don't need. It is really an act of charity to use a full-service broker when you go generic. Haven't you already given enough at the office?

At this point you might want to go back and look again at Figure 4 (p. 71). It will give you a flashback overview of the whole how-to process, a checklist of what's involved. Hopefully, the steps in the chart and their proposed flow are now clearer.

A Note About Financial Institutions and the Generic Strategy

A lot has been said about private investors and how they can benefit from the Neglected Firm Effect by applying the Generic Stock Investment Strategy. But what about financial institutions? Can they also use this approach?

As we shall see in the next part of this book, where

the reasons for the Neglected Firm Effect will be discussed, financial institutions are to a large extent responsible for the information deficiency that creates the Neglected Firm Effect. The amazing Blue Giants Paradox will be presented there. But can financial institutions themselves apply the Generic Stock Investment Strategy and benefit from it like small investors? Or, perhaps because of their size and other constraints and restrictions, is this particular avenue closed to them?

The answer depends on the size of the financial institution. As a rule, the larger it is, the less successfully it can apply the Generic Stock Investment Strategy, mainly but not exclusively because of liquidity problems. For a more complete discussion of the factors constraining financial institutions, wait for the next chapter.

Semi-Generic Stocks: A New Investment Opportunity in Prospect?

There is no reason why the generic idea should be foreign to investment companies as it has been in the past. One possibility would be to create mutual funds of generic stocks that manage generic portfolios for small investors. Investment companies, particularly the comparatively small ones, can create a professionally diversified, efficient portfolio of neglected stocks. They have better tools to do it effectively than small investors, and they also possess greater financial resources to invest in a larger number of generic stocks.

Just a moment! screams the skeptic in you. The product that these "generic funds" will sell will be nongeneric. Won't they charge for their services? And won't it soon be the case that because the underlying securities they invest in are being followed, they will by definition stop being generic? This particular vehicle will take them and their investors nowhere!

Yes and no. Generic mutual funds obviously will charge management fees for their services. Therefore, their portfolios will be more expensive than the sum of their components. But this higher price might be well worth paying, for some investors who prefer to go generic halfway, by applying the Generic Stock Investment Strategy with some professional help.*

What I am proposing here is a new concept that might be called the Semi-Generic Investment Strategy: invest in generic stocks *indirectly* by using the professional services of small mutual funds, or closed-end investment companies that specialize in generic stocks. These funds would perform the search, the pruning, the diversification, and the portfolio maintenance for small investors—for a fee. The essence of this idea is that whatever these investment houses do as investment managers, they should try to stick to the generic area by making continual portfolio adjustments in an attempt to first precede, and then to ride on and benefit from, the popularity flow, by selling when a stock becomes popular, but never

---

*Another alternative is to make the investment decisions and to manage the portfolio *yourself*, but with some specific advice from an investment service that specializes in generic stocks like the one in reference [6].

staying at the fancy brand-name marble towers. That's what will make them unique compared with existing investment companies.

This, in fact, would be the first time that one would be able to buy a share of stock in a whole orphanage instead of bothering to adopt several neglected orphans, one by one.

The generic idea is not an either/or approach. It can be in between. When you buy a private brand product, like a supermarket chain's private brand beans or, Sears's private brand appliances, you in fact go semi-generic. While you don't pay for a national brand name, you also don't buy a true no-name generic product. You in fact go in between. You let the retail organization select, package, and monitor generic products for you. To some extent the retailer operates as your *generic agent*. You, of course, pay for it. The price of the product is somewhere between that of the true generic product and the brand-name one. But the information deficiency and the resulting estimation risk are also in between. And you also benefit from the fact that your "agent" can buy in large quantities and you cannot. This is the idea of semi-generic stocks, or a generic mutual fund investment.

Food for Thought 10: Can the Really Big Ones Go Generic? The Winning Record of a Huge Money Manager That Went Semi-Generic

Do the large institutional investors have a choice? Can they benefit from the Neglected Firm Effect or are they bound to worship the blue and leave the gray (and the resulting gold) for others?

Let's have a look at the nation's eleventh largest stock market investor, Batterymarch Financial Management. This is an interesting exception to the rule, showing that even for big investors blue and gray can fit, at least within limits, and result in considerable success. In 1983 Batterymarch Financial Management managed a portfolio of stocks of $11.1 billion. It has 134 large pension and endowment clients, with a minimum account of $10 million. Still, for this year it had a return of 30.3 percent, outperforming the Standard and Poor's average by 8 percentage points. This has been the best showing among the giant money managers. And 1983 was not an exceptional year. This was the third straight year that

Batterymarch beat the market. The company's performance has been outstanding before as well, for example in both 1976 and 1977 when its returns were a stunning 20 percentage points above the S&P.

Clearly, Batterymarch is a rare phenomenon among the big institutions. It is highly entrepreneurial. In fact, it does not behave its size. Unlike other large money managers, the company is owned and run by one person, Mr. Dean leBaron. As a recent article in *The Wall Street Journal* (December 8, 1984) stated, "He *is* Batterymarch." Under him the company has just twenty-nine employees— a very small number for a company like this.

The penalty/reward factor for taking risks is clearly different here than in most other large institutional investors. Mr. leBaron is directly rewarded for successfully taking an unconventional approach. *The Wall Street Journal* estimates that he keeps sixty percent or more of gross revenues, which in 1983 totaled $27.8 million. That, according to *The Wall Street Journal,* probably makes Mr. leBaron the highest paid money manager in the United States. So, in spite of size, the motivation factor here favors a more entrepreneurial approach.

Furthermore, "The whole firm is organized to challenge conventional wisdom," according to the *Journal.* Mr. leBaron is a classic "contrarian"—buying stocks that are out of favor with other investors. For instance, companies with six straight quarterly earnings declines and a dividend cut. The kinds of investments that can benefit from favorable surprises and not be hurt by unfavorable surprises (see more about stock prices and good and bad news in "Food for Thought 13," p. 204).

More specifically, among the strategies responsible for Batterymarch's winning record, *The Wall Street Journal* mentions, "investing in small to medium companies that were selling at low price-earnings ratios and were less

than 10 % owned by other money managers"—i.e., neglected stocks.

Mr. leBaron was smart, however, not to apply the generic idea to his whole portfolio all the time. Flexibility,
open-mindedness, and continual switching from one
policy to another are distinct characteristics of the company's investment strategies, all clearly contributing to
its winning record.

"Most ideas tend to decay," Mr. leBaron says. "The
market discounts the effects of widely held views. We're
dedicated to finding new ways of doing things. We flee
from things that have been successful. I'm still fasci-
nated by the quest, and the uncertainty."*

I couldn't have said it better as a pitch for the generic
stock idea. This great success story suggests that at least
within limits even large financial institutions can benefit
from the Generic Stock Investment Strategy.

*As quoted in *The Wall Street Journal,* May 8, 1984.

PART III
WHY DOES IT WORK?

Why Is the Why Important?

Why is it necessary to spend time on the reasons for the Neglected Firm Effect? After all, to drive a car, you don't need to know how it works. But this attitude can lead to a lot of trouble when the car breaks down. The more you understand the underlying mechanism that makes a tool work, the better use you can make of it.

In this part the following questions will be discussed: Why does the Neglected Firm Effect exist? What is the market mechanism behind it? Why is the Generic Stock Investment Strategy expected to work? Why for some and not for everybody? How is it related to the Small Firm Effect? Why does it prevail over time and not disappear like so many other self-destructing market processes? What can we expect for the future? Why are there reasons to believe that the Neglected Firm Effect is the underlying determinant for several other astonishing market anomalies like the January Effect or the Low P/E Anomaly, that are so hard to explain?

Some commonly expressed skepticism of gloomy thoughts about the market will also be considered: Is the whole thing just a gamble? A continuous game of chance in which greedy investors are lured and pushed by the powerful brokerage industry and where on average the only winners are the game promoters and not the players? What's the role of the generic idea in this respect? What are the chances for small investors? And how does the key notion of market efficiency fit in?

Factors Determining Stock Prices: The Basic Theory

In order to understand the economics behind the Neglected Firm Effect, it is important that we first review a basic question: What determines share prices of stocks?

The starting point is almost obvious: the price of a share reflects the value that investors attach to the company's future earnings and/or dividend payout. Future earnings can be expressed in terms of the current earnings and the anticipated growth rate into the foreseeable future.

But how do investors decide on the price that they are willing to pay for the anticipated earnings?

Here the answer is not that simple. To start with, it depends on what other investment opportunities are available. Investors use the return on other investments as a discount rate, or benchmark, to estimate the price of the expected earnings flow.

Look at Figure 10, opposite. It summarizes the three key factors determining share price. The price of a share depends first on the anticipated earnings, which reflect the market consensus concerning the future growth rate of the firm. Clearly, the brighter the future prospects of the firm, the higher the share price. For example, when investors expect the competitive position of the company to improve, the stock price rises, and vice versa.

FIGURE 10
Basic Stock Valuation Principles

Share Price Goes Up with the

1. Anticipated Increase in the Growth Rate of the Company's Earnings or its Dividend Payout

2. Decline in the Perceived Risk

3. Decline in Expected Return on Other Investments (as Approximated by Expected Decline in Interest Rate)

The second key factor is the risk, or uncertainty, associated with the earnings. The greater the perceived risk, the lower the price investors are willing to pay for the expected earnings stream.

The third factor is the opportunity cost, or the return on other investments. The greater the cost in terms of other opportunities forgone, the lower the share price. Thus, when Chairman Paul Volcker of the Federal Reserve loosened monetary policy in July 1982 and the interest rates on bonds and other money market investments dropped, the stock market moved up sharply. Especially when Mr. Kaufman told the world that this was indeed what was going to happen. The basic rule is that share prices always move in the direction opposite to interest rate expectations. When the interest rate is expected to go up, stock prices go down.

The Role of Risk

Risk is a key variable in investment. At this point you might be intrigued by the loose use of the word *risk*. You might want to hear more about its real meaning, its impact on investment decisions, and how it is measured.

We have already seen that risk refers to anticipated fluctuations in stock prices and returns. Recall that risk can be separated into essentially two components. The first is the general risk faced by the market as a whole, sometimes called the systematic risk or the beta risk. This is what we see as fluctuations in the trend of the market, a bullish market going up, a bearish market coming down. Practically all stocks are affected by this risk. The second type of risk is specific to the company (and to some extent to the relevant industry). This is called the unsystematic risk because it is not related to the market system as a whole, but is unique to the company. Recall that in a well-diversified portfolio, the price fluctuations unique to one company are offset by the price fluctuations of other companies in the portfolio. The same applies for fluctuations in dividends. The investor experiences only the systematic risk.

The traditional theory of investments as summarized by the widely accepted Capital Asset Pricing Model (CAPM.) is that share prices and returns are affected primarily by (a) the going riskless rate that represents the alternative return that investors can get without assuming risk, and by (b) an additional return, over and above the risk-free rate, which is a *risk premium* or compensation for taking risk. The higher the risk, the higher the additional return over and above the riskless rate.

What risk should be compensated for? According to the CAPM only the systematic—market-related—risk, which cannot be diversified away. The other part of the risk, the unsystematic—company-related—risk, can be, and is assumed to be, diversified away by most investors. Therefore, it does not deserve any reward in terms of higher return. All prices in the market are assumed to be determined by supply-and-demand factors to create a return that is consistent with the riskless rate and the level of the systematic risk. No more and no less. Thus, if for some reason return on a certain stock is above the "justified" one supply-and-demand forces will start to operate; there will be excess demand for this high-return stock, the price will go up and the return down. This process will continue until the price has reached its equilibrium level, which is—you guessed it—the "fair price" that yields exactly the "justified" return. According to the CAPM the market is always in equilibrium or close to it. Why? Because rational investors who always have all the information will discover any abnormal opportunity immediately and will move fast to correct any disequilibrium.

This in a nutshell is the story of risk and return, at least according to the currently most accepted model in finance. While this model has been widely criticized in recent years as being too simplistic and unrealistic, no *plausible* alternative has been suggested.

To understand better the main notion of the CAPM, consider the following example. What should be the long-term return on General Motors stock according to this model?

First, investors have to be compensated for not investing in a riskless investment. This is the immediate, most basic, opportunity cost. Everybody can invest in, say, a money market fund. So, this is the base. Let's take here 8 percent as a long-term average.

Second, for taking the additional risk of investing in a common stock rather than staying safe and warm under the stable wings of some money fund, additional return is required. Otherwise, nobody will invest in equity. General Motors happens to have a beta coefficient of about .90 (check in *Value Line Investment Survey* [18]). Recall that the beta coefficient measures the volatility of a stock vis-à-vis the market as a whole. (This is an index of the systematic, or market-related, risk, when the benchmark is 1.) So, General Motors is a bit less volatile than the market as a whole. (If it had a beta coefficient of 1, its expected volatility would have been exactly that of the market; with a beta of 1.4, higher than the market.) Therefore, according to the CAPM the risk here is slightly lower than for the market portfolio and so should be the return. Now, let's assume that the long-term expected return for the market as a whole is 12 percent. According to the CAPM the market-related risk premium of any stock should be the difference between the expected market return and the risk-free rate multiplied by the beta of the stock (in our case $[.12 - .08] \times .90 = .036$ or about 4 percent). This 4 percent is the market-related risk premium for General Motors. This should be added to the base of the riskless rate, 8 percent, resulting in total long-term expected return for General Motors of 8 percent + 4 percent = 12 percent. That's what the model tells us.

What about the risk of General Motors *itself:* the fluctuation in returns of the stock over and above the market as a whole? No compensation is expected for this (unsystematic) risk, because it can be and is assumed to be diversified away. Investors can and should invest in other securities that will cancel out this company-related risk. The market pricing mechanism does not compensate you for your mistakes, according to the model. It's your problem if you do not diversify as you could and should. The market pricing system is based on rational behavior.

Food for Thought 11: Can Market Inefficiency Explain the Higher Return on Generic Stocks?

Recall the discussion about market efficiency and the hypothesis that the neglected segment of the market is probably less efficient (see "Food for Thought 2," p. 39). However, a less efficient market does not imply a continuous above-average return. When a market is inefficient some stocks are overpriced and others underpriced. Consequently, market inefficiency cannot fully explain the Neglected Firm Effect. Further explanation has to be found.

This is important and most relevant for us. When a market segment is inefficient better opportunities exist for investors if they have the ability to identify the underpriced winners and avoid the overpriced losers. Here inefficiency spells opportunity. If you are good at it, you'll make a return even above the average for the neglected stocks group as a whole. Again, you won't get something for nothing, you'll have to earn it.

Why Generic Stocks Perform Better

Now that we have some basic theoretical understanding of the factors that affect share prices and returns according to the going theory, we are ready to consider the central question of this part's discussion: Why do neglected securities outperform those that are highly researched? It can't be market inefficiency, so what is it?

One way to answer this question is to consider which of the three key factors that affect stock prices are most likely to be influenced by the level of analyst attention and/or institutional holding—i.e., expected growth, risk, *or* riskless rate (e.g., the interest you can get on a short-term Treasury bill). Alternately, we can ask ourselves whether the Capital Asset Pricing Model is inapt with respect to neglected stocks. It is possible that modern investment theory as represented by the CAPM can explain the pricing process of only *most* companies in the market, but not that of the neglected segment, which might operate in a different way because of lack of information about it.

It is clear that the opportunity cost, or the return on other investments, cannot be the reason for the superior returns on neglected stocks. This factor is identical for all stocks. Why should neglected stocks be impacted differently? The superior return must be related to some dimensions of risk: a compensation for taking it or for the effort to reduce it. Our discussion so far has suggested that the poverty of information (in quantity, quality, accessibility) reduces the price that investors are willing to pay for stocks, and hence, raises the return on neglected stocks.

But it's not clear yet how a lack of information can be used to rationalize lower prices on neglected securities. After all, the missing information could be either positive or negative in its potential impact on the securities' value. For any large number of stocks it is reasonable to assume that over the long run about half of the information will be positive and half negative. The net effect should be no effect, and it does not matter if the stocks are neglected or popular. Is it possible that the whole concept of generic stocks, which had been borrowed from the product markets, is inapplicable to the financial markets and, therefore, fatally flawed?

Let me tell you a story. Imagine a widespread media strike all over the country. There are no newspapers: *The New York Times* is not being sold, there is no *Wall Street Journal,* even the small-town newspapers are mute. TV and radio stations are dead. Even Louis Rukeyser is quiet. The only sources of information are some sputtering shortwave radios that talk mostly about the rain in Spain in foreign languages and . . . rumors, lots of rumors.

What would happen to stock prices in this hypothetical situation?

Of course, the extreme information deficiency under these conditions would cause *all* stock prices to go down. The mere fact that investors have no information or have less information affects stock prices. The point is that at least to some extent generic stocks permanently reside in an environment of information deficiency. As long as they are neglected, their prices are lower than other, nonneglected companies.

Going back to the list of factors that determine stock prices, we can conclude that it is not the opportunity cost, or the expected earnings growth rate, that generates higher returns on neglected stocks, but rather the perceived risk, which is affected by information deficiency. The lack of information on neglected securities makes the future earnings more difficult to predict. There must be some compensation for the lack of information and for the required effort to correct for it. Otherwise no investor would ever touch such a foggy stock. This compensation is the generic premium.

The skeptic is now on his feet again, saying: Didn't you find in your research that even after adjusting for risk, neglected stocks outperformed the nonneglected ones? Haven't you told us that the whole point is that the Neglected Firm Effect persists even *after* adjusting for risk?

True, the Neglected Firm Effect persists after adjusting for the *traditional* measures of risk (like total volatility in return or the beta coefficient). But, don't forget, these measures are historical measures, they relate to the past and are used without regard to their level of reliability or the credibility of the information on which they are based. Think how we arrive at these traditional risk measures. The bookkeepers crank out numbers that are assumed to be equally reliable for all companies. These numbers are then mechanically taken to calculate measures of risk (among other things) and we assume that investors are so naïve as to do the same.

One of the most successful businessmen in the world,

Baron Rothschild, said recently in a TV interview, "I hate figures, they confuse me." It is not that numbers and the whole quantitative approach are not needed for effective business decisions. Of course, they are. However, numbers can be misleading. One has to know what the numbers represent and to make sure that they are comparable.

The key point is that in the usual procedures for risk adjustment—the beta coefficients, volatility measures, financial ratios, and all the rest—no account is taken of the potential difference between the historical measures and the perceived, forward-looking risk as seen by investors, that is, the difference between ex post and ex ante risk. At a low level of information, the perceived risk may be much greater than the one that is a reflection of the bookkeeper's numbers as traditionally measured. In fact, these numbers might not be very meaningful in the generic area. Investors realize that this is the case and are less willing to accept the various traditional measures of risk at their face value. In fact, to some extent investors don't really believe in the traditional risk measures in this particular case. This accounts for the lower price and higher return of generic securities.

Information Deficiency and Estimation Risk

Since the idea of information deficiency is so important, not only for understanding the generic phenomenon but also for an effective practical use of it for improving market performance, let's try to make it even clearer by introducing a key concept critical for the generic stock idea. This is the concept of *estimation risk*.

Because of the lack of information, there is a lot of estimation risk on top of the measured historical risk associated with neglected stocks. In fact, the traditional risk measures when applied to neglected-generic stocks are fuzzy, or not very reliable in their information content. That's why it is so important to use a lot of cross-checking, diversification, and judgment. Apparently, investors, and consequently the market pricing mechanism, take into consideration, not only the risk measures themselves as represented by the numbers, but also the quality of these numbers. For generic stocks the quality is low. Simple common sense tells us that the relevant overall risk perceived by investors—the one that actually determines stock prices and returns—is the sum of the measured risk and the estimation risk.

Another way to look at it is to say that the estimation risk is the risk associated with the risk measures themselves. Something like the instability of the instability measures. The more generic a stock is, the less reliable are the traditional risk measures, and the higher is the estimation risk. According to this notion, the Neglected Firm Effect is simply a premium that investors get for taking higher estimation risk and a reward for coping with it—a combination of *estimation risk premium* and *entrepreneurial premium*.

A simple extreme example might help to illustrate this point. Imagine a case of the ultimate neglected stock: a small unknown company that is not even public, struggling to introduce a new product. Except for its single enthusiastic, zestful, and tireless owner, nobody really knows or cares what's going on: zero information, no audited financial reports, no outsiders monitoring. There is not one single financial institution holding the stock or assessing its performance. The venture capital guys are watching—but still from a distance. The company hardly has a name. Even for such a company, if you push hard you can produce a whole series of financial ratios including a complete set of the traditional risk measures. Would you consider this set of financial ratios to be comparable to an identical set for, say, IBM? Does the market? Of course not! The estimation risk here is huge.

Can the Estimation Risk Be Estimated?

Now is the time for the pragmatic in you reluctantly to inquire, Can the estimation risk actually be quantified? Or is it an imaginary concept that exists only in the eye of the beholder?

This is a fair question and not easy to answer.

I don't know of any way to directly measure estimation risk. But there are ways to approximate it. One way is to look at the spread in analysts' earnings forecasts. This is a measure of consensus among analysts regarding the company's future. The less information you have, the less is the consensus among analysts, and the higher the estimation risk. When the underlying information is not reliable you have to rely more on judgment, hunches, and bits of information collected from all over, all of which lead to a wider spread of opinion among analysts To the investor who attempts to evaluate the company the picture is fuzzy and blurred. Therefore, lack of con sensus among analysts can be used as an approximate measure for estimation risk.

Think of a short-term government note, maturing tomorrow. Here you have the ultimate case of perfect information; practically everything relevant to determine the return of this informationally clean financial asset is known with certainty. What will the consensus be among analysts regarding the future return in this case? No doubt, perfect! All analysts will agree and come up with the exact same evaluation. Full consensus.

Now, compare this level of consensus with the name-less company that I mentioned earlier. The consensus there will be much smaller or perhaps nonexistent. The range of future earnings estimates will probably be from a huge loss all the way to high profits.

There are simple statistical measures to estimate consensus. One can use the relative variance in analysts' earnings estimates, or the coefficient of variation. Two financial information services calculate analysts' consensus measures for thousands of companies on a current basis. We have mentioned them before. They are IBES [7] and Zacks [22]. Thus, an approximate measure of information deficiency and its outcome—estimation risk—exists and can even be compared and cross-checked using two independent sources.

The next question is so obvious that both the skeptic in you and the pragmatist are patiently waiting for it to pop up by itself: What is the empirical evidence? Does the evidence as actually observed in the market support the hypothesis that estimation risk as measured by the variance in analyst consensus increases with the degree of neglect?

The answer is yes, and very decidedly so. Our research findings clearly indicate that the more a company is followed by analysts and/or held by financial institutions, the more of a consensus you find, implying a lower level of estimation risk; and vice versa: The more a company is neglected, the less is the consensus, which implies a higher level of estimation risk. Thus, for example, the level of consensus regarding the expected earnings of IBM should be much higher than that for

Yatom Corporation. If indeed such relationships can be found for a large and representative number of companies in a statistically significant way, it would confirm the hypothesis that generic stocks have a higher level of estimation risk.

Results of empirical research clearly support this hypothesis. In a study to be published in a forthcoming issue of the *Journal of Portfolio Management,** a highly significant negative correlation was found between the level of consensus among analysts and degree of neglect. This indicates a reverse relationship between popularity of a stock and its level of estimation risk; the more a stock is followed by analysts the lower is the information deficiency and the resulting estimation risk; and the opposite is true for neglected stocks. The message is clear: generic stocks encounter more confusion.

What Determines Degree of Neglect?

Another key question is of course what determines analysts' attention?

Interestingly, this question connects the Neglected Firm Effect with the Small Firm Effect. Recall that no plausible explanation for the observed consistent superior

*Avner Arbel, "Generic Stocks, Information Deficiency, and Market Anomalies," scheduled for publication in the fall of 1985.

returns for small firms has been offered. The Small Firm Effect is still one of those market mysteries that nobody knows how to swallow. Small firms as a group seem to be a better investment. Everybody knows about it and still the self-correcting process is not strong enough to erase these abnormal returns. Does this suggest that there is a simple trading rule (buy small companies) to beat the market consistently? It does not make sense.

However, consider the following explanation, which is directly related to the critical question just asked: What in the first place determines analysts' attention?

No doubt, several factors are involved here, but perhaps the most important one is the clientele. Most security research and analysis is done by and for financial institutions, which are the leading factor in the market. Consequently, the investment policy of financial institutions is extremely important in affecting the degree of coverage and level of attention that a company gets. Stocks that they consider to be "investment quality" (actually or potentially) get a lot of analysts' attention. The others get much less. This is clearly related to company size, or "market cap." in the institutional jargon ("cap." for capitalization, i.e., the market value of shares outstanding).

As we have already mentioned more than once, as a rule financial institutions do not invest in small firms. There are several reasons for this. Some relate to the legal constraints imposed on financial institutions by different regulatory agencies. Others have to do with self-imposed constraints and the economics and psychology of managing large portfolios by salaried managers. They cannot be and have no incentive to be as entrepreneurial as you can.

In a recent article in the *Financial Analysts Journal* we presented this point as follows:

Institutions, mutual funds, banks, and money managers are somewhat like giraffes. Both for good structural reasons and as a matter of preference they concentrate on the tall trees in the investment forest, ignoring the underbrush. Structurally, institutions face several difficulties in investing in firms with small capitalizations. First, the typical size of an institutional investment could affect the price, hence the liquidity, of low capitalization, thinly traded securities. Second, such an investment would frequently result in more than 5 per cent ownership, requiring an insider's report to comply with Securities and Exchange Commission regulations. Third, the holding could quickly become large enough to necessitate managerial input, which often falls outside the institution's area of interest and expertise.

With respect to their preferences, institutional fund managers may not want to take the greater risk perceived to be associated with small firms. They are expected to follow a prudent investment policy, which frequently means doing what everybody else does. And many institutions require that an investment yield dividend income, and few small firms do.*

*Avner Arbel, Steven Carvell, and Paul Strebel, "Giraffes, Financial Institutions and Neglected Firms," *Financial Analysts Journal,* June 1983.

The Interaction Between Company Size and Neglect

Let's now take our analysis one step further, and try to understand the relationship between company size and neglect. Since most of the financial research is done by institutions or to satisfy their needs, the lack of institutional interest results in less research, less monitoring, and consequently an information deficiency in the market segment in which financial institutions are not active. Thus, company size is an important factor in creating the phenomenon of institutional neglect and the resulting information deficiency.

The rest of the story is clear. We have said it before: small neglected companies are in fact generic in the true meaning of the term—large estimation risk, no monitoring, and no stamp of approval. The observed higher return for small firms is in effect a generic premium, or estimation risk premium plus entrepreneurship premium. The Neglected Firm Effect, at least to a large extent, explains the Small Firm Effect. They are two sides of the same coin.

It should be kept in mind, however, that size is not the only factor determining neglect. There is a high, but less than perfect, correlation between size and neglect. (In the *Journal of Portfolio Management,* study mentioned on page 170, I found a correlation coefficient of between $-.40$ and $-.70$ between size and neglect depending upon the measure of neglect used. This means that stocks of small firms are mostly generic but not all generic firms are small.)

The finding that size is not the only reason for neglect is consistent with common sense and with what we continuously observe in the market. Recall that even the largest oil companies slid in popularity in late 1982 and the beginning of 1983 when energy prices went down and the energy crisis monster was reduced to a more realistic size. At the other end of the spectrum, some small high-tech companies are highly followed now. The popularity flow can start with a firm that is still small, resulting in a small nonneglected company.

On the other hand, it is equally important to realize that small size and neglect interact. The absence of analysts' attention is much more critical in the case of a small firm. Therefore it is not surprising that the highest returns are generated by firms that are both small and neglected.

The interaction between size and neglect is related to the notion of declining value of incremental information. The idea is simple and intuitively appealing: the more information one has about something, the less is the value of additional information on the margin.

Small firms have usually less of a past record of performance, and whatever exists is less meaningful. Consequently, the starting level of information is low. Given the principle of declining value of incremental information on the margin, additional information provided by analysts is more critical in the case of small firms. The opposite is also true: lack of current analyst follow-up is more damaging for small firms than for big companies. This implies that the reward for lack of information—the information deficiency premium—should be larger for small firms than for large firms. This is indeed what we found in our empirical investigation: the actual return in the market has been higher for small neglected firms than for large neglected firms.

The following chart in Figure 11 conceptually summarizes the process of interaction between the Small Firm Effect and the Neglected Firm Effect.

FIGURE 11
Information-Driven Explanation for the Neglected and the Small Firm Effects

> **Companies (Mostly But Not All Small) Are Neglected by Financial Institutions.**

↓

> **Consequently, They Are Neglected by Analysts.**

↓

> **This Results in Greater Information Deficiency, Less Monitoring, Higher Estimation Risk.**

↓

> **Consequently, Neglected-Generic Stocks (Mostly But Not Only of Small Companies) Are Priced Lower.**

↓

> **This Results in the Greater Returns for Neglected-Generic Stocks.**

↓

> **Since Information Deficiency is More Critical for Small Companies, the Returns for Small Neglected Companies Are Higher Than for Large Neglected Companies.**

An Explanation for the Low P/E Anomaly?

Can the factors behind the Neglected Firm Effect also explain the Low P/E Anomaly? The Low P/E Anomaly relates to another astonishing market phenomenon: the consistent, outstanding performance of low P/E stocks for many years. A large portfolio of stocks selected on the basis of the P/E criterion alone, with no other screening at all, will perform extremely well. Practitioners and academicians have been challenged by this phenomenon because, like the Small Firm Effect, it seems to suggest a simple trading rule to beat the market. It implies that you get something for nothing and therefore it is hard to explain how it can survive over time without being wiped out by profit-seeking investors.

However, if you incorporate the informational aspects of neglected stocks that we have just discussed, the explanation of this phenomenon becomes obvious. Typically, neglected-generic stocks have a low P/E. Thus, the outstanding performance of low P/E stocks is in effect a variation on the same theme: a reflection of the Neglected Firm Effect. The higher returns here are largely a generic premium.

In a recent study presented to the Atlantic Economic Society at its international convention in Rome (March 1985),* I specifically tested the following hypothesis:

> Degree of neglect (generic) and not company size, or the magnitude of the P/E ratio per se, is the underlying factor in generating higher returns.

A data base of about one thousand companies for a period of five years (1978–82) was compiled.†

Table 8 presents correlation coefficients between return (including dividends) and company size (as measured by market capitalization), price/earnings ratio, and three different measures of neglect. These findings reflect the results of pooling, a technique that combines cross-sectional and time series correlation analysis for close to five thousand observations (the one thousand companies studied for five years).

You can see that the results largely confirm the hypothesis stated above. Degree of neglect and not company size or the magnitude of the P/E ratio as such generates higher returns. Interestingly, in our sample no Small Firm Effect is detected. On the contrary, a statistically significant positive correlation coefficient between company size and return indicates that, across all

---

*The study results will be published in the *Journal of Portfolio Management* [2].

†Correlation and multivariable regression analysis have been used as the main tool to identify meaningful relationships between the variables. In addition techniques like Stepwise Analysis and the Goodnight Maximum R^2 Improvement Technique have been employed to assess relative importance of variables. In order to capture possible non-linear relationships logarithmic specification of the variables has been tried, as well as different lagging structures to capture delayed effect.

TABLE 8 Correlation Coefficients Between Return and Size, Price/Earnings Ratio, and Degree of Neglect*

| | Return | Company Size | Neglect | | | P/E |
			(a) Inst. Hold. No. of Shares	(b) Inst. Hold. Pct. of Equity	(c) Inst. Hold. Weighted†	
Return	—	.0403 (.007)	-.0900 (.0001)	-.1001 (.0001)	-.1008 (.0001)	.0393 (.0320)
Company Size		—	.737 (.0001)	.392 (.0001)	.719 (.0001)	.029‡ (.1100)
Neglect:						
(a) Inst. Holding No. of Shares			—	.602 (.0001)	.849 (.0001)	.0411 (.037)
(b) Inst. Holding Pct. of Equity				—	.501 (.0001)	.067 (.037)
(c) Inst. Holding Weighted†					—	.0611 (.0008)
P/E						—

*Correlation coefficient is a measure of association between the variables in question. It ranges between 0 to 1. A coefficient of 1 indicates a perfect direct association; when one variable goes up the other is expected to go up in the same magnitude. A coefficient of 0 indicates no association between the two (independent behavior). The larger the coefficient within the range of 0 to 1 the stronger the association. Negative coefficients (like − .5) indicate inverse relationship, i.e., when one variable goes up, the other goes down, or vice versa. Again, the larger the coefficient, the stronger the inverse relationship. Level of significance is presented in parentheses (in terms of prob. > R under HO: RHO=0) usually .05 or lower is considered to be statistically significant.

† A combined measure of (a) and (b).

‡ Statistically insignificant even at the 10-percent level.

Source: A. Arbel, Journal of Portfolio Management [2].

size groups, larger companies performed better.* Still, a highly significant Neglected Firm Effect is apparent. The smaller the institutional interest, the higher the return. This is true for all three measures of institutional neglect. Not surprisingly, there is a high correlation between company size and degree of neglect (.39 – .74 depending on the measure of neglect used). However, the correlation between the two is less than perfect, indicating that some large companies are neglected and some medium-size and small companies are popular. This finding combined with the relationship between size and return, and neglect and return, suggests that firm size might act as a surrogate for neglect but is not the underlying factor in generating higher return. This conclusion was previously confirmed in other studies in which the Neglected Firm Effect was detected, when firm size was held constant, but no Small Firm Effect was apparent when degree of neglect was held constant.

The P/E anomaly is apparent though it is less strong (i.e., less statistically significant) than the Neglected Firm Effect. The study's key finding as far as the P/E ratio is concerned is the high negative correlation between degree of neglect (all three measures) and P/E. Neglected stocks tend to have a lower P/E. The data show no significant association between company capitalization and P/E (see Table 8). Combined, these results suggest that informational factors relating to the degree of neglect, rather than company size, are responsible for the higher returns of low price/earnings stocks. It is the generic

---

*Given the analytical tool used, i.e., linear regression analysis, this does not exclude the possibility that the extremely small companies performed well. Our findings simply imply that higher return is not generally associated with smaller size across *all* size groups.

premium that you get here, with all the costs involved and not something for nothing.

Actually, this analysis supports the practical conclusion, previously discussed, that low P/E ratios can be taken as proxy for neglect. This is a handy measure of neglect that according to this study captures part of the Neglected Firm Effect.

I prefer more direct and explicit measures of neglect but, in their absence, the P/E ratios can be used as proxies.

The Amazing January Riddle Revisited

We have mentioned before another market anomaly that is still unexplained: the January Effect. Can the idea of differences in information deficiency, consensus, and estimation risk help to explain this phenomenon, too? Here the situation is more involved.

Every year for the last twenty-two years, with just two exceptions, market prices have gone up markedly at the period starting on the last day of December and ending on the fourth trading day in January. The average return of these five days alone, in the last eighteen years, was 5 percent on the New York Stock Exchange and 6.3 percent on the Amex. This is equivalent to more than 260 percent and 328 percent annualized.

This phenomenon amazes Wall Street practitioners and

market theoreticians alike not only because of the obvious profit implication but also because (once again) it contradicts existing theories. For example, the January Effect is inconsistent with the market efficiency premise: you again have here a simple trading rule to beat the market consistently. It is also contradictory to the premise of rational investor behavior: investors should have wiped it out by larger participation in the January feast. It is not so much the January Effect itself that attracts researchers' attention but the challenge of better understanding the market. This phenomenon irritates market observers. According to the existing theories it simply cannot happen and, if for some unknown reasons it does, it should immediately be expunged by profit-hungry investors trying to take advantage of it.

You might think it possible that most investors don't know about the January Effect and consequently only the select few who are informed take advantage of it, and that this might not be enough to cancel it out.

This is not very likely. On December 24, 1982, just before the critical days for investors to effectively participate in the coming January party, *The Wall Street Journal* devoted its most widely read column "Heard on the Street," to our research on the January Effect. It presented the whole story on a golden tray for investors to grab if they so desired. Amazingly, the January Effect is stronger than the publicity that could have ruined it. The effect strongly persisted again in January 1983.

The question of course is, Why? Why does the January Effect occur in the first place, and how can it persist over time?

I know of at least eight professors of finance, some well-known names in the field at top universities, and many Ph.D. candidates, who are now working hard to answer these questions. There have also been several research proposals submitted to various funding organizations to request support for extensive research in this area. As of now, the jury is still out and the recent "Vas Ist Das?" cry of despair of Professor Roll (see p. 42) is still appropriate.

We were first tempted to believe that the January Effect is related to the Neglected Firm Effect by the findings presented in Table 9.*

What is so striking about these findings is that they clearly indicate that the January Effect is much stronger for neglected companies. In fact, after adjusting for risk, nonneglected companies demonstrate a reverse January Effect (see last column in Table 9). These findings are consistent with previous results of Professor Roll and several other researchers showing that most of the outstanding January returns are traced to small firms. Given the high reverse correlation, previously discussed, between size and neglect, the similarity in results is not surprising. Thus, a new puzzle has been added to the January riddle; the question now is, not only Why in January? but also Why mainly neglected companies? Surprisingly, this new dimension of the phenomenon can help to untangle it.

Four explanations for the January Effect can be offered, all consistent with the evidence of a stronger effect for neglected firms. Let's briefly present these explanations one by one. You will immediately realize that they are not mutually exclusive.

---

*These findings are the result of a joint study with Professor Paul J. Strebel and Steven Carvell of the State University of New York at Binghamton. The study is based on a different data base. See discussion on data and methodology including empirical definition of grouping companies by degree of neglect in an [2].

TABLE 9   Average January Returns and Risk-Adjusted Returns By Degree of Neglect 1971–1980

	Average January Return (%)	Average January Return Minus Average Monthly Return During Rest of Year (%)	Average January Return After Adjusting for Systematic Market Risk (%)
(a) S & P 500 Companies:			
Highly Researched	2.48	1.63	−1.44
Moderately Researched	4.95	4.19	1.69
Neglected	7.62	6.87	5.03
(b) Non-S & P 500 Companies:			
Neglected	11.32	10.72	7.71

Source: A. Arbel, *Journal of Portfolio Management* [2].

The first, and the most widely cited, explanation is related to taxes. Some investors sell stocks at the end of the year in order to benefit from tax losses. Others sell to report capital gains for the current year rather than the following year. These sales depress stock prices in an artificial way toward the end of December. Since this has nothing to do with the underlying economic strength of the company in question, the depressed stocks are soon discovered by other investors as bargains. They start to buy them, which pushes prices up—creating the January rally. This process is much more substantial for neglected companies. Many financial institutions, such as pension funds and endowments, are tax-exempt. Others are less involved in the tax-loss sales because they comply with special tax arrangements (e.g., insurance companies), or because they report their results in gross, pretax, terms anyway (e.g., mutual funds) and the risk of being caught in tax-related transactions is higher for them than the expected benefit. Consequently, institutions as a whole are less involved in the end-of-year tax-selling game. It is expected, therefore, that stocks that aren't held by institutions and thus are less analyzed are more affected.

Furthermore, the neglected-generic stocks as a rule have a thin market. Therefore, even a comparatively small volume of trading substantially affects the price, much more than in the case of popular stocks.

The second explanation can be called the Santa Impact. It relates to end-of-year cash flow needs. Some of the cash needed to finance the annual Christmas buying spree comes from selling stocks. This, like the tax factor, creates a selling pressure, especially from small investors who liquidate part of their savings. Thus, again stock prices go down for reasons unrelated to their fundamental worth. The bargains are soon picked up by other investors, creating the big jump at the turn of the year. Once more, this factor is much more critical for smaller, neglected companies because of their smaller market capitalization and the resulting higher price volatility.

Third, many money managers tend to dress up their portfolio at the end of the year to make their highly visible year-end portfolio look more prudent and palatable to clients and analysts. For many portfolio managers the generic investment opportunities were fine as tempting, hidden sins. But, exciting as they were, they have to be swept under the rug for the big end-of-the-year report, which is supposed to be full of brand names that everybody approves. Here, again, we have a temporary selling pressure that is motivated by nonfundamental factors. The prices of the rejected stocks are artificially depressed and then corrected, in a jump, in the early January rally.

All these explanations make sense and probably have

some contributing role in creating the January Effect. However, two problems cast doubt regarding their completeness in accounting for the phenomenon. First, they all imply a large price decline just before the January rally. There is no clear, convincing evidence that this is indeed the case. Second, and much more serious, they cannot explain how the outstanding seasonal market performance could persist over time for so many years. If profit-seeking investors knew about the January Effect, wouldn't their own market activity wipe it out once it is widely followed? It seems that additional explanations are needed.

The fourth explanation hypothesizes that informational factors related to seasonality in estimation risk are the main reason for the turn-of-the-year rally. More specifically, I propose that seasonality exists in information quantity, accessibility, and perhaps as important, in the level of acceptance by investors.

Most companies have fiscal years that end in December. Information from the annual reports starts to leak or is closely predicted at the turn of the year in an effort to precede the official announcement. The same is true of dividend and other distribution announcements, which are usually considered to be relevant signals to investors. Furthermore, the turn-of-the-year period is traditionally a period of performance evaluation. Assessments of market gainers and losers are published in practically all popular finance and investment periodicals. The success and failure stories of companies as well as investment managers are highlighted. Moreover, not only does more and better information exist around the end-of-the-year period but the information is more accessible. In fact, part of it is actually pushed on investors by companies, money managers, and the media in the flood of the "year that was" reports.

The seasonality in information dissemination is expected to affect all stocks, but it is much more critical for neglected stocks, because of the previously discussed declining marginal value of information. In the case of many really neglected companies, the period surrounding the annual report is often the only time in which any new official (audited) information reaches the investment public. In contrast, the effect of incremental information for highly researched securities is weaker, given the high level of information already existing. Thus, the corresponding decline in estimation risk and required return would be greatest among neglected-generic firms, resulting in the highest price increases. Traffic signals are more important in foggy areas.

Finally, there is another factor that contributes to the outstanding January performance of neglected stocks and in turn helps to explain the January Effect as a whole. This has to do with the beginning of the popularity flow for the more successful neglected stocks. Recall that lists of market leaders, stocks that outperformed all other stocks, are widely published and followed at the end of the year. For many years most of the top market leaders have consistently been neglected stocks. In recent years close to 60 percent of all popular business publications have published a market "winners" list *only* at year-end. We also found that about 57 percent of all shareholders of the New York Stock Exchange are exposed to at least one year-end winners list. Furthermore, even larger numbers of investors are attracted from among the more relevant group who invest most in neglected-generic stocks, namely, those of higher income brackets of $30,000 or more.

Thus, at the end of the year, more than at any other period, the top performers, most of them neglected stocks, attract the attention of a substantial number of investors and analysts. This triggers the beginning of a popularity flow. The obscure winners, the hidden successes, are suddenly in the limelight. Their merits disclosed, they become more popular and price increases immediately follow. This is in fact a period of epiphany and not just of the divine.

In sum, while all stocks would enjoy the effect of the seasonal decline in estimation risk, the impact on prices of neglected stocks should be stronger. The strongest effect, however, would be on stocks of successful neglected companies because of the additional impact of the start of the popularity flow.

If this scenario about seasonality in quantity, quality, and accessibility of information is indeed correct, it all should be reflected in a lower observed variance in analysts' forecasts (that is, more consensus) during January, indicating lower estimation risk, which in turn explains the higher January prices (remember, when you have less information deficiency, prices go up—other things being equal).

Furthermore, the observed decline in the mean variance forecast (i.e., the proxy for information deficiency) should be stronger for neglected-generic stocks, which in turn would explain the outstanding January performance of neglected stocks.

Using the Institutional Brokers Estimate System (IBES) computerized data base for the six-year period of 1976–81, we have analyzed monthly measures of analyst consensus segmented by degree of neglect, for an overall universe of close to sixty thousand observations.

The results are presented, in Figures 12 and 13 for the most widely followed stocks (followed by more than fifteen analysts) and for neglected stocks (followed by only three to five analysts), respectively.* What do we see in

---

*Companies followed by a smaller number of analysts were excluded in order not to distort the variance measures.

FIGURE 12
Popular Stocks: Coefficient of Variation
in Analyst Forecast by Month, Average 1976–1981

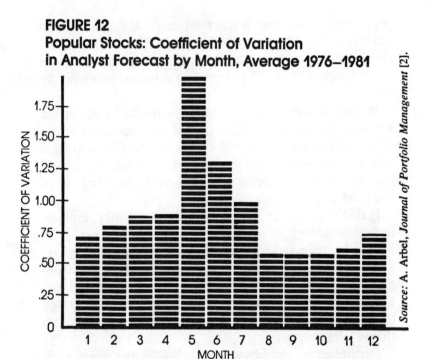

Source: A. Arbel, Journal of Portfolio Management [2].

this graph that looks like a bunch of midtown sky-scrapers on the horizon of some unknown, crowded city?

The findings confirm seasonality in analyst consensus over the year. Clearly analysts tend to agree more in January because of the better quantity and quality of in-formation. The variance in earnings forecasts (i.e., the proxy used for information deficiency and estimation risk) is low in January for both neglected and popular stocks, but it is by far the lowest for the former; the decline in information deficiency is the strongest for neglected stocks (compare Figure 12 with Figure 13).

Given this finding, as well as the notion of declining marginal value of information mentioned above and the low starting level of information for neglected compa-nies, a rise in price as a result of better information in

FIGURE 13
Neglected Stocks: Coefficient of Variation
in Analyst Forecast by Month, Average 1976–1981

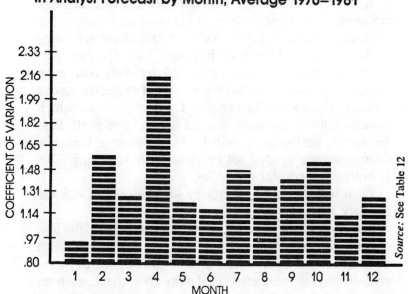

Source: See Table 12

January is expected for all stocks but it should result in a much higher jump for generic stocks than for the brand name ones.

This is in fact what happens in the market (see again Table 9 p. 183). The January returns for the highly neglected companies were almost five times larger than for the highly followed companies. Other researchers have found the same phenomenon. They labeled it the "January size effect." Our analysis suggests that here again it is not size but information that matters.

How can investors participate in the January feast? The answer is quite straightforward: Put your money in a large, diversified portfolio of neglected stocks before the end of the year, hold them for five to ten days, and sell.

If what happened in the past happens again, the return should be pretty substantial.

What about screening? Isn't it better to avoid high-risk companies? The answer here is the same as for any other neglected stock; whatever we have said about screening in the previous chapter applies here, too. The past performance measures just presented indicate that even without screening, any large portfolio of neglected stocks will do, thanks to the benefit of diversification, which cancels out the company-related risk in large portfolios. However, performance will be even better if high-risk companies are weeded out by some basic screening. This is critical for smaller portfolios.

What will happen if everybody starts investing with the January Effect in mind?

It will disappear. The more participants it gets, the less effective it becomes (so, keep this book to yourself). But if, as in the past, financial institutions continue to be restricted in their neglected/small firm investment, such an outcome is less probable. As basic economics tells us, when barriers to entrance exist, the self-correcting process is impaired.*

---

*To the amazement of everybody, just before the book went to the printers, the January Effect happened again in 1985. See a vivid description in *Time* magazine (February 4, 1985, p. 40).

Why Does the Neglected Firm Effect Survive Over Time? Will It Disappear in the Future?

This brings us to another interesting question: Why does the Neglected Firm effect survive over time? How could a trading strategy that results in abnormal returns exist over time without being fully exploited and in effect milked to death by profit-thirsty investors. Using the logic of those who were bred on the market-efficiency premise, the crucial argument can be posed: If a trading strategy to beat the market is found, it can survive only as long as it is not widely used. Once spread it is self-destructing. And, no doubt, it will spread because investors are rational; they want to make money. So, if it works, it is bound to be destroyed, and if it doesn't, who cares? Finding a satisfactory answer to this argument is clearly critical—the moment of truth for any claim for an effective strategy to improve market performance.

The key point in rebutting this argument is the realization that in using the Generic Stock Investment Strategy you do not get something for nothing. This point should be crystal-clear to every potential investor in generic stocks. Over the long run you can expect higher returns for investing in generic stocks. But there is a cost attached to it. The generic stocks are coming wrapped with information deficiency. As emphasized in the previous chapter, you have two choices regarding the estimation risk. You can try to reduce it or hopefully even eliminate it by doing research yourself and by diversification. This obviously has a cost. Or, alternatively, you can elect to live with the lack of information and take the risk. This also has a cost.

Clearly—and this is what most investors in neglected stocks do—you can combine the two. Do some of the research yourself and diversify—eliminate part of the estimation risk, and live with the rest.

Look at it from the point of view of what is now called in financial literature "agency cost theory." In the generic area, nobody is working for you to collect, check, analyze, and update information and you don't pay for it. No agents are monitoring companies' management performance for you and again you don't pay. The generic companies could be, and sometimes are, an orgy for insiders. So you the outsider had better be careful.

The point is that whatever you do when you go generic there is a cost. And when cost is involved a trade-off exists. It is cost versus benefit, and it is for you the investor to decide. The benefit might be largely equal for all investors but not the cost. Some investors have specialized knowledge about an industry, a company, or perhaps even inside information. Some are better at analyzing, or have better "intuition." Certain investors might have higher alternative costs—better and more important things to do—and others might decide that the whole thing is not for them.

The Neglected Firm Effect survives over time because there is no free gift here but rather the usual trade-off between cost and expected benefits. If different peo ple have different preferences regarding the trade-off, then the generic stocks with their higher average return can exist forever side by side with the distinguished, name-brand darlings. They are simply not the same, so why should the price tag, or its outcome, be the same?

It seems that there is indeed a future for Jack's Ocean View Motel as well as for Holiday Inns, for no-name generic soup, as well as Campbell's and for the stock of Yatom Corporation as well as for IBM. They can live together side by side forever. . . .

It still may not be clear why financial institutions do not take advantage of the Generic Stock Investment Strategy—and by doing so eliminate the phenomenon altogether?

Look at the following logical structure, says the skeptic. It is based upon three assumptions and one conclusion that is their immediate outcome.

Assumption 1.   Outstanding returns can be made by investing in neglected stocks, as has been shown to us.

Assumption 2.   Financial institutions have a lot of money; they are the major participants in the financial market and they want to maximize their returns.

Assumption 3.   Financial managers know about the Neglected Firm Effect and the generic idea.

If these assumptions are true, then there is only one conclusion: Financial institutions should extensively invest in neglected stocks. By their doing so, neglected stocks would stop being neglected and the whole Neglected Firm Effect would disappear, carrying with it into oblivion the generic idea, the Small Firm Effect, the January Effect, and all the rest. Everything would collapse and the market would go back to normal.

A key assumption is missing in the straightforward, logical structure just presented here. In order for it to be true, one has to assume as well (a) that financial institutions are free to explore all segments of the market as they wish and (b) that they actually do so. We have to assume no constraints, external or self-imposed, on their investment policy. Fortunately for the generic stock idea, very substantial market barriers do exist, preventing financial institutions from investing in certain securities. These constraints create the Neglected Firm Effect in the first place and prevent its disappearance.

What are these constraints? I have mentioned some of them before, where the factors determining analyst attention have been discussed (see p. 170). Institutions, because of their size and their traditional conservative role in financial markets, prefer to be involved in the brand-name area of the market (which they themselves create) and avoid the generic area. Given their size, the liquidity that small, neglected companies offer is insufficient. Institutions need the dividend income that generic companies typically don't provide. They want to avoid direct involvement (imagine Apple Computer Corporation in its infancy managed by a pension fund) and the problem of being considered insiders by the SEC and others. Moreover, both government regulations and tradition prevent them from taking the entrepreneurial approach so important for investment in generics.

Consider a related point: the money manager's own point of view. Many institutional investment managers often avoid the generic stocks simply to protect themselves. They often prefer to play it safe and avoid generic stocks even when the potential gains are high enough to justify the investment from the standpoint of the financial institution that they manage. Let's be realistic about it. Managers of many financial institutions have higher-level goals—such as their own corporate survival—over and above the goal of maximizing the market value of the portfolio that they manage. And for many managers, corporate survival often means investment in brand names. When your portfolio is nongeneric it is easier to rationalize when something goes wrong. Who can blame you for doing what everybody else is doing?

In sum, financial markets in the real world are less than perfect. This point is important for investors to realize. It opens interesting opportunities.

Let's add a fourth assumption to the skeptic's list and see what happens to his logical structure:

Assumption 4.   Market barriers exist. Institutional investors are not free to invest in small and/or neglected companies, or for other reasons consistently choose not to do so.

Does the previous conclusion regarding the collapse of the Neglected Firm Effect and the disappearance of all the rest hold now? The answer is no, it does not. This brings us to the Blue Giants Paradox.

Food for Thought 12: The Blue Giants Paradox

Several references have been made in this book to the megadollar investors, the large financial institutions, the blue giants. It might be interesting to have a closer look at the biggest of them all—the nation's largest stock-market investors. Who are they? And how was their market performance in recent years?

In Table 10 you will see a list of the ten largest stock portfolio managers, data on the size of their portfolios, and most interestingly, their equity returns.

In spite of their huge resources, unlimited research potential, and excellent connections, the performance of the giants did not measure up. The average performance

TABLE 10   The Nation's Ten Largest Stock-Market Investors

Manager	Stocks Managed at Year-End 1983 (in billions of dollars)	1983 Equity Returns (in percent)
1. Bankers Trust	23.8*	22.5†
2. J. P. Morgan	22.0	23.5†
3. Citicorp	18.0	21.1†
4. DLJ/Alliance Capital Management	15.7	21.0
5. College Retirement Equities Fund	14.6*	25.3
6. Capital Group	13.7	23.0†
7. Marsh & McLennan (Putnam/Eberstadt)	12.1	12.1
8. Mellon National	11.4	24.8
9. Metropolitan Life/ State Street Research	11.4	18.8
10. Wells Fargo	11.2*	23.02†
Average		21.5
Standard & Poor's 500 Average		22.4

*More than half passively managed index funds
†Applies to tax-exempt assets only
Source: The Wall Street Journal (May 8, 1984).

of the ten biggest, as a group, was in 1983 almost 1 percentage point below the Standard and Poor's 500 average for the same period (21.5 percent versus 22.4 percent).

This is the Blue Giants Paradox. The most managed portfolios performed worse than an unmanaged portfolio. These results are unbelievable at first. They clearly indicate that one could have applied a simple sampling procedure to approximate the S&P 500 stocks and invested in an unmanaged portfolio. This can be done by hiring less than one thousand dollars' worth of basic statistical advice or, even cheaper, by randomly selecting twenty to thirty stocks. As mentioned earlier, research evidence shows that this is more than enough to proxy the market portfolio. The portfolio's performance would have been better. Truly much better, taking into consideration the huge saving on management fees estimated to be more than a billion dollars a year, paid to the hundreds of hardworking portfolio managers who were beaten by an unmanaged portfolio that a computer (or a blindfolded monkey) could have selected.

Are there any exceptions among the ten biggest investors? Not really. The best performer was College Retirement Equities Fund with equity return of 25.3 percent which is just about 3 percentage points better than the S&P 500. Interestingly, most of the funds managed by CREF were invested in passively managed index funds or in fact were unmanaged.

Was 1983 an exception? Not at all. The literature is full of evidence that consistently shows the same results for practically every time period checked. Together they show that the nation's largest institutional investors have not outperformed unmanaged portfolios, even before allowing for management fees.

What is the reason for this poor performance? The answer by now should be obvious. The largest investors did not benefit from the generic premium. They are bound, or choose to, operate in the established, brand-name segment of the market. Because of external and self-imposed constraints, they have been limiting themselves to the established larger stocks, those that have minimum estimation risk and hence lower return.

Furthermore, on average, the return of the biggest investors was even lower than the S&P 500. This is to be expected because even the S&P 500 universe contains several stocks that are off-limits for the big institutions. These stocks are consequently neglected and offer generic premium but not, of course, for those who passed them over.

This is a fascinating paradox. The big guys create the generic premium that they cannot enjoy. If they were to attempt to profit from it, it would disappear. A stock market tragedy—for the big, square guys, that is. But quite a comedy for small investors and smaller institutions: an opportunity for the entrepreneurial investor.

The Generic Cycle and the Popularity Cycle: The Dynamic Process

Now we can take the discussion one step further and try to understand the dynamic process in the market. What is the process that creates first a neglected stock and later a generic premium? This process can be represented by the *generic cycle* and the *popularity cycle*. They both have their own momentum and a tendency to accelerate. Let's discuss them one at a time and see how they are connected.

As a consequence of institutional constraints, a generic cycle is created. This idea is summarized in Figure 14.

This generic cycle starts with, and depends upon, the

FIGURE 14
The Generic Cycle

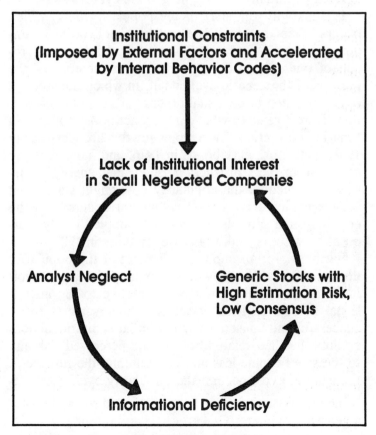

constraints that force institutions to avoid the small-capitalization, neglected segment of the market.

Given that most financial research is done by and for financial institutions, the lack of institutional interest leads to analyst neglect. Limited coverage by analysts, in turn, generates an informational vacuum characterized by the high estimation risk and low consensus typical of generic stocks. This creates even higher perceived risk and makes the generic set even less adequate for institutional interest. As a result, even less research is done, and so on and on . . . the cycle continues.

What eventually breaks the generic cycle?

It stops with the start of the popularity flow, which occurs when the stock is eventually recognized as underpriced or a "bargain." This usually happens as a result of one of two things: first the momentum of the process of the generic cycle itself, in which the stock is overly rejected in the usual process of market overreaction. Here I refer to what Street practitioners often call "market correction." Examples for this are Chrysler in 1981, New York City bonds in 1976, and more recently stocks from the construction, steel, and energy industries. Or, second, the popularity flow might start when some significant positive development occurs with the company that attracts attention. Example: Tandy Corporation with its Radio Shack computers in 1982.

Furthermore, an important element of the popularity flow process is that growth in company size usually follows success, making it more attractive to big institutional investors. Thus, when a company starts to be successful and consequently the initial institutional constraints that had related both to the perceived risk and to the size become less and less binding, the reverse of the generic cycle occurs: the popularity cycle (see Figure 15).

FIGURE 15
The Popularity Cycle

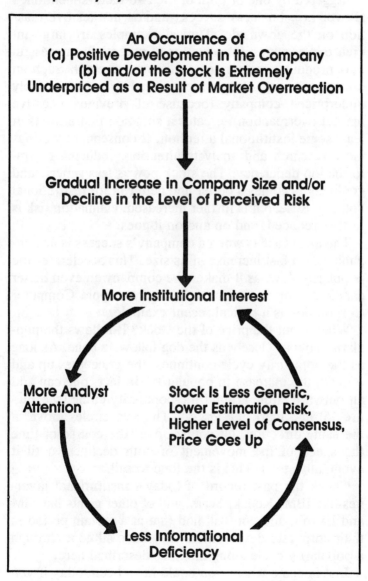

An Occurrence of
(a) Positive Development in the Company
(b) and/or the Stock Is Extremely
Underpriced as a Result of Market Overreaction

Gradual Increase in Company Size and/or
Decline in the Level of Perceived Risk

More Institutional Interest

More Analyst
Attention

Stock Is Less Generic,
Lower Estimation Risk,
Higher Level of Consensus,
Price Goes Up

Less Informational
Deficiency

As this simplified diagram shows, the popularity cycle is triggered by one or both of the two factors mentioned above: i.e., business success and/or market overreaction on the downside. Typical examples are large increase in earnings, introduction of potentially successful new products, merger, or a takeover attempt. Such an occurrence, especially when related to an excessively underpriced company (because of previous negative market overreaction), creates a situation that attracts at least some institutional attention. It consequently brings more research and analysts attention, reducing the information deficiency. The stock now is less generic and gradually becomes a better and better fit for institutional holding. Research is further increased, estimation risk is further reduced, and on and on it goes.

The ideal case is when a company's success is accompanied by a fast increase in its size. This accelerates the popularity flow, as it makes the company an even better candidate for institutional investors. Apple Computer Corporation is a typical recent example.

What about the price of the stock? It follows the popularity flow as closely as the dog follows a bone. As long as the popularity cycle continues, the price goes up and up with the increase in popularity. In fact, one can add an outward circle around the popularity circle (see Figure 15) and mark it "Price." The two circles move in the same direction. Of course, over the course of time the speed of the movement of both declines, until it eventually stops. This is the time to sell.

Check the past record of today's institutional favorites like IBM, Kodak, Sears, and of other giants like GM and Exxon, and you will find that at a certain period in their corporate development they have all gone through a popularity cycle along the lines described here.

Just imagine where you could have been today if you

had bought some of these stocks at their generic stage.

This demonstrates once again the rules of the generic game:

—Catch a stock before it starts its popularity flow, that is, invest in really neglected stocks.

—Make sure that each stock is not a lemon and that it won't become a nebbish; therefore screen.

—Diversify. You want to avoid the generic trap; you can never tell for sure, in advance, a true generic stock from a lemon or a nebbish.

—Don't overdo it. You shouldn't go as far as Spokane, Washington (see p. 131).

—Finally, don't forget that it all continuously flows, so manage your portfolio: when the popularity flow stops or if it does not materialize, sell and switch.

This is the essence of the Generic Stock Investment Strategy.

And finally, fear not. The phenomenon will probably not disappear. Whenever you get something for something rather than something for nothing, the self-correcting process does not work.

Actually, an absence of higher return for the entrepreneurial exploration of the neglected area of the market would be more of an anomaly than its presence.

The generic premium is simply a fair deal.

Food for Thought 13: Information Shocks and Big Price Changes. Are All Stocks Equally Sensitive to Bad and Good News?

At any given moment, prices of stocks represent all existing expectations. Typically, a very large up or down move in price occurs when some unexpected development arises that significantly changes the existing expectations. If investors know a stock will go up tomorrow, you can be sure it will go up today. The unforeseen is really what matters. This is what investment theory tells us.* But consider the difference between favored and unfavored stocks in this respect.

When a stock is favored, investors are expecting good news or at least they don't expect bad news. Consequently, when good news occurs for a widely favored stock, it cannot move the price much because it has been expected and therefore impounded in the price. But if bad news comes forth, the stock is bound to go down

---

*For a good discussion, see B. J. Malkiel, *Random Walk Down Wall Street* (New York: Norton, 1975).

substantially because negative developments are indeed unexpected for a favored stock.

In fact, if the stock has been very popular, bad news might hit like a ton of bricks. Given the size of their holdings, when institutional investors become nervous about any of their stocks a devastating snowball effect can result. The giants usually stick together. When they don't like the taste of something, they dump it.

Take the example of Digital Equipment (or DEC as it is widely known)—the nation's largest minicomputer maker and second only to IBM in the computer field as a whole. Clearly a brand-name stock, a darling of the institutional clan. Or at least it used to be until October 18, 1983, when the unexpected happened. DEC announced a huge decline in earnings of 73 percent. The megamoney guys were furiously disappointed. They reacted like enraged bears. No doubt, the big bucks have a lot of power. In three days the stock was massacred, plunging from about 100 to 67. This slaughtered about one third of the company's market value. Call it institutional revenge, a common phenomenon when institutional favorites turn bad. This is less likely to happen with neglected stocks that the big guys dismissed as useless untouchables to start with. After all, to be disappointed you need at least to have had some expectations at the outset.

When a stock is out of favor, the megadollar investors don't expect good news or anticipate negative developments. If good news peeps out, it is really unexpected and the price jumps. The process is further accelerated by the thin float (small number of shares outstanding), typical for small/neglected companies. This can explain why neglected stocks usually move up in price in jumps compared with popular stocks that move more gradually (see discussion on pp. 43–50). Furthermore, given the existing unfavorable expectations for neglected stocks, nothing much happens when the expected bad news turns out or when no news transpires. Typically, the hibernating turkeys simply continue to hit the hay, as anticipated, with little if any decline in price.

Thus, with different states of the world, the favorite might stay favorite, which is okay, or become an unfavorite, which is bad. The neglected can stay unfavorite, which is okay (remember, you have bought them at a low price *because* they were unfavored), or become favorite, which is good. Sum it up and compare the results.

EPILOGUE
SOME POSITIVE SKEPTICISM ON THE WAY TO RICHES

Now that the entrepreneurial approach to investment and the generic idea is pretty clear, you might be wondering about the bottom line of all this. Not only about the generic stock idea but about the whole market phenomenon. From time to time investors get some gloomy thoughts about the market. Especially when they are not doing too well. Haven't you brooded occasionally along the following depressing lines:

Isn't the stock market the biggest gambling place in the world, where the whole huge investment and brokerage industry with its sexy research establishment and pushy brokers basically sell dreams of fast wealth to greedy people? And, in the process, provide roller-coaster kicks and not much more?

The Wall Street Journal recently quoted a private investor who said that playing the market is the same as playing Las Vegas: "There's no point thinking about it. You just do it." Isn't this investor indeed one hundred percent correct? Perhaps making money in the stock market is purely a matter of luck—and all the analysis and the commentary that surrounds it is merely hoopla, make-believe, the biggest bubble in town with absolutely no basis in reality.

Some investors, when really hit by market melancholy, might push this point even further:

The stock market is actually worse than the horse trading market. Over there at least you know that you trade horses. In the market frequently you cannot distinguish between a horse and a donkey. Often you don't have enough information and many times donkeys are sold to you as horses. All investors, with practically no exceptions, hope to buy a horse for the price of a donkey and ride it fast to the land of riches and happiness. This cannot be possible, at least for the majority.

It is hard to dismiss these dark thoughts; they hold more than just a grain of truth.

True, the market process is extremely complicated. We are dealing with the future. We trade in perceptions. In most cases the odds are unknown, and the process is loaded with emotions: greed and fear and often apathy in between. It is not only that the target continuously moves; we move too as our attitude changes. Clearly, it is very hard to hit with such conditions.

But perhaps this does not represent the whole picture.

The key for success on Wall Street is in trying to predict the future, using whatever relevant information you can get. When it comes to predicting what's going to happen, companies and the economy differ from the dice, because their future is less dependent on a random process of pure chance. Luck, important as it is, is only part of it. The better you are at discovering new opportunities, assessing future performance, screening and checking, the better your chances are for success. But you have to do it before everybody else does.

Many investors, owing to human nature, and the big investors, because of market barriers, tend to cluster together and to plow and replow the same area, leaving the periphery an unexplored wilderness. If you are shooting for above-average returns, you have to leave the warmth of the herd. Very few are willing, but you may be one who is.

So cheer up. Remember, wherever there is a reward for honest hard effort and especially when the reward is high as it is here, there is hope!

The Generic Stock Investment Strategy shows that you

cannot only resist the pressure of the investment establishment but also take advantage of its weakness, the barriers that restrict its flexibility.

What you in fact can do is to carefully sniff out and uncover your own treasure. True, it is not for everybody, but what is? And, in this particular case, luckily so. If it were for everybody it would not exist.

References

[1] Edward Altman, "Financial Ratios Discriminant Analysis and the Prediction of Corporate Bankruptcy," *Journal of Finance,* September 1968.

[2] Avner Arbel, "Generic Stock, Information Deficiency and Market Anomalies," *The Journal of Portfolio Management,* forthcoming in the fall of 1985.

[3] Avner Arbel, Steven Carvell, and Paul Strebel, "Giraffes, Financial Institutions and Neglected Firms," *Financial Analysts Journal,* June 1983.

[4] Avner Arbel and P. J. Strebel, "Pay Attention to Neglected Firms!" *The Journal of Portfolio Management,* Winter 1983.

[5] Dow Jones & Company. *Dow Jones News/Retrieval.* P.O. Box 300, Princeton, NJ 08540. Tel.: 1-800-257-5114.

[6] The Generic Stock Investment Service. P.O. Box 6567, Ithaca, NY 14851.

[7] Institutional Brokers Estimate System (IBES). *Monthly Summary Data.* Lynch, Jones & Ryan, 325 Hudson Street, New York, NY 10013. Tel.: 212-243-3137.

[8] B. J. Malkiel, *Random Walk Down Wall Street.* New York: Norton, 1975.

[9] Media General Financial Services, Inc. *Industriscope.* P.O. Box C-32333, Richmond, VA 23293. Tel.: 804-649-6569.

[10] Moody's Investors Service, Inc. *Moody's Bond Record.* 99 Church Street, New York, NY 10007. Tel.: 212-553-0300.

[11] Moody's Investors Service, Inc. *Moody's Handbook of Common Stock.* 99 Church Street, New York, NY 10007. Tel.: 212-553-0300.

[12] Richard Roll, "Vas Ist Das?" *Journal of Portfolio Management,* Winter 1983.

[13] Standard & Poor's Corp. *Standard & Poor's Guide.* 25 Broadway, New York, NY 10004. Tel.: 212-208-8769.

[14] ———. *Standard & Poor's Earnings Forecaster.* 25 Broadway, New York, NY 10004. Tel.: 212-208-8769.

[15] ———. *Standard & Poor's Stock Guide.* 25 Broadway, New York, NY 10004. Tel.: 212-208-8769.

[16] P. J. Strebel and A. Arbel, "The Neglected and Small Firms Effects," *Financial Review,* XVII 4, November 1982.

[17] John Train, *The Money Masters.* New York: Penguin, 1981.

[18] Value Line, Inc. *Value Line Investment Survey.* 711 Third Avenue, New York, NY 10017. Tel.: 212-687-3965.

[19] ———. *Value/Screen.* 711 Third Avenue, New York, NY 10017. Tel.: 212-687-3965.

[20] *Wall Street Transcript.* 99 Wall Street, New York, NY 10005. Tel.: 212-747-9500.

[21] William O'Neil and Co. *Daily Graphs.* P.O. Box 24933, Los Angeles, CA 90024. Tel.: 213-820-2583.

[22] Zack's Investment Research. *The Icarus Service.* 2 North Riverside Plaza, Chicago, IL 60606. Tel.: 312-559-9405.

Index